OUT of ISLAM

OUT *of* ISLAM

CHRISTOPHER ALAM

Charisma
HOUSE
A STRANG COMPANY

Most Strang Communications/Charisma House/Siloam/Front-Line/Realms products are available at special quantity discounts for bulk purchase for sales promotions, premiums, fund-raising, and educational needs. For details, write Strang Communications/Charisma House/Siloam/FrontLine/Realms, 600 Rinehart Road, Lake Mary, Florida 32746, or telephone (407) 333-0600.

Out of Islam by Christopher Alam
Published by Charisma House
A Strang Company
600 Rinehart Road
Lake Mary, Florida 32746
www.charismahouse.com

Unless otherwise noted, all Scripture quotations are from the King James Version of the Bible.

Cover design by studiogearbox.com

Library of Congress Cataloging-in-Publication Data

Alam, Christopher, 1954-
  Out of Islam / Christopher Alam.
    p. cm.
  ISBN 1-59185-890-9 (paper back)
    1. Alam, Christopher, 1954- . 2. Christian converts from Islam
--Biography. 3. Conversion--Christianity.   I. Title.
  BV2626.4.A39 A3 2006
  248.2'46092--dc22

                                  2006009069

First Edition

06 07 08 09 10 — 9 8 7 6 5 4 3 2 1
Printed in the United States of America

To Britta,

Immanuel,

Victoria, and

Gabriel

Acknowledgments

⌇

I WANT TO THANK my fathers, mentors, and friends in the faith who have loved me, encouraged me, and made a difference in my life. First, the late Rev. Kenneth E. Hagin Sr., always "Dad" to me. Then Harald Bredesen, Reinhard Bonnke, Ray McCauley, Billy Joe Daugherty, John Nuzzo, Stanley Hofwijks, Mark Butler, Sam Hinn, Jerry Horst, Bill Lee, Bruce Eilenberger, Sam Smucker, Kong Hee, Joseph Prince, Enevald Flaaten, Tony Cooke, Nicholas Mavondo, William Lamhno, Kenneth Hagin Jr., Ulf Ekman, and so many others whose names I cannot put here because of lack of space.

Contents

Prologue

AN UNFINISHED SERMON

⎯⎯⌇

SOMETHING WAS IN the air.

I could feel it.

The words "Are you ready?" slipped from my lips and roared from the platform speakers and across the grass field. My eyes traced the scene before me. A short distance away sat thousands who gathered in a soccer stadium not to cheer on a team but to listen to a man behind a pulpit.

I was the man.

"Returning as He promised, Jesus is coming again. Are you ready?"

Uncountable eyes stared back at me.

Overhead the sun pressed down its rays, warming the late afternoon and washing the stadium in light. The weather in Blagoevgrad, Bulgaria, presented no distraction. Blagoevgrad, once a bastion of Communism, once a showpiece of a political philosophy that had no tolerance for the very message I brought to this service, was now the center of an evangelistic crusade. Communism was now a dark memory, and the city was open to a presentation of the gospel. I had the honor of presenting it.

Those who lived in New Testament times called this land

Macedonia. The city lies nestled at the foot of the Rila and Pirin Mountains and is the major municipality of the region. Twenty-five villages ringed the city limits. Those who sat in the stands had come from city and town—one in four of the city's population was present, and each sat in stony silence.

"Jesus is coming again. Are you ready to meet Him?"

I had delivered a simple message about Jesus, one I had given many times, but something was different. Something was in the air—and something was in me.

In my core, at the center of my being, the ever-present passion I felt for Jesus flashed to a roaring blaze. I had proclaimed a message about the life of Jesus, about His death, about His triumphant resurrection that changed the world. Now I came to the climax of the sermon—the imminent return of Christ.

I never finished.

"Are you ready?" I asked again, then paused.

The silence was palpable, heavy.

Then a sound.

A noise.

Someone in the stands shouted. Then another. Before I could utter my next words, the crowd was on its feet. They surged forward, pouring over the railing that separated the seating from the field like a river over the crest of a waterfall.

Their noise rose in thunderous tones. The platform upon which I stood vibrated, resonating with the voice of the congregation.

They flowed forward like the tide, crossing the distance between the seats and platform in moments. Hands shot up, reaching skyward as if attempting to touch the face of God.

Tears rolled down their cheeks, and their voices rose in loud prayers—prayers for mercy, prayers of acceptance. At the platform many knelt, heads bowed, souls sobbing.

My sermon was over before I planned. God moved ahead without me. I stood still as a statue as I watched the sight unfold before me. I was at a loss for words, which is not something that happens often. The Holy Spirit touched not one, not a hundred, but thousands of listeners.

What could I say? What could I do? What could I add?

The same emotion that had swallowed the crowd inundated my own soul. Meaningful words were gone from my mind. I surrendered the microphone to a Bulgarian pastor and asked him to lead the crowd in a salvation prayer.

In this moment of high drama, in the midst of this outpouring of the Holy Spirit, I felt broken in the most marvelous way. I stumbled to the back of the platform, hiding myself behind some chairs. Inside me emotion boiled, then erupted in sobs; sobs turned into prayer.

While thousands were finding salvation at the front of the platform, I was facing my own sense of unworthiness to be part of such a stunning display of God's power.

"Thank You, Lord Jesus," was all I could mutter. I have learned that the more meaningful the emotion, the more simple the prayer. "Thank You for saving me when I was down and lost; thank You for bringing me so far and allowing me to see Your power and Your glory. You have brought me such a long way...such a very long way. Thank You, Lord. Thank You."

The words came with tears and with the stiff realization that the man who hunkered down behind folding chairs in prayer was far removed from the person he used to be—the person I used to be.

The service continued, and I returned to my duties. My sermon may have been cut short, but God wasn't finished. A paralyzed man, carried in a blue blanket by his family, rose to his feet and began to run through the crowd. Others, just as crippled, stood, walked, and jumped, some for the first time in their lives. Blind eyes began to see, deaf ears opened, and miracles abounded—all in a stadium in the heart of a former Communist city.

As always, Jesus had the final word, not just in this city or in this crusade, but in my life—something no one would have anticipated.

OUT *of* ISLAM

That night in my hotel room, I lay on my bed, my spirit soaring and my thoughts directed to God. In the dark of that evening, I thought about what I had seen, what I felt in the pulpit, and the long road that led me here.

The man that lay on the bed in the hotel room was not the same man who decades before began life in a Muslim home.

Chapter 1

MUSLIM ROOTS

I AM CHRISTOPHER ALAM, descendant of Muhammad, of Ishmael, and of Abraham.

I was born on March 29, 1954, in a Muslim home in Pakistan. My father's side of the family was Hashemite Arabs from the Middle East. Members of my grandfather's extended family still live in Jordan and Lebanon. People called us by the honorific title "Shareef" (or "Sayyid" by some), a term used only for those directly descended from Muhammad, the founder of Islam.

Muhammad had only one son, Ibrahim, who died in infancy; consequently, the family line runs through his daughter Fatima, who became the wife of Ali, Muhammad's young cousin and the first convert to Islam. Because I was a direct descendant of Muhammad, people respected me, treating me as a "holy" person. Most considered me superior to them. I, however, knew my own heart and could never escape the fact that I was nothing more than a sinner.

One of my uncles had a copy of our family tree. It traced our lineage back to Muhammad and from there to Ishmael, Abraham's son, and, of course, to Abraham himself. We were proud of our heritage.

My father was a hero, decorated for gallantry under fire during a covert operation conducted while he was with the ISI. I was proud of him.

My grandfather was a religious man, having made the pilgrimage to Mecca. The British government decorated him for his service to the Crown and granted him a title. He was renowned for his hobby of herbal medicines. He traveled far and wide collecting rare plants and herbs for his remedies and lived a disciplined, healthy lifestyle. He outlived four wives and died at the astonishing age of 106. I must clarify here that he never had more than one wife at a time. While Islam dictates that a man may have as many as four wives simultaneously (because that is how many wives Muhammad had), my grandfather chose not to follow the practice. Muhammad had at least thirteen wives, and he married his last wife Aisha when he was fifty-seven and she was just nine years old.

My father was born when my grandfather was seventy and was the seventh and final child from grandfather's fourth and last wife. Growing up, I remember meeting so many uncles, aunts, and cousins that I lost count. I still run into people who claim to be my cousin, people I have never met. Because of the age difference between my father and his oldest siblings, I have nephews and nieces older than my parents. They addressed me as "uncle" whenever we met. At times it was confusing.

For example, when I was a cadet at the Pakistan Air Force College, one of my nephews was a fellow cadet. He outranked me. Whenever we met, I would come to attention, salute, and call him "sir." When he gave me orders, he did so as he would others of lower rank but also made certain to address me as "uncle." He knew that when we were out of uniform I would be his senior because I was his uncle.

My family left the Middle East and settled in what was then British India. My father held the King's Commission, and he was an army officer and graduate of the Royal Indian Military Academy in Dehra Dun, India. Upon the division of British India into India and Pakistan, the old British Indian army split as well. The officers and men had the choice of joining either the new Indian Army or the new Pakistan Army. My father, being Muslim and seeing no future for Muslims in the new India, opted to join Pakistan and continue his service there. That is where I was born.

As with most military families, we moved to a new military base every three years or so. My childhood was an ever-changing chain of military bases spread throughout the country. My father was an artillery officer, but he also served two tenures as a senior commanding officer in the famous Directorate for Inter-Services Intelligence (ISI), the organization that worked with the CIA to create the Taliban and to arm Afghan and Arab fighters battling the Soviets in Afghanistan. One of those Arab commanders was a man by the name of Osama bin Laden.

My father was a hero, decorated for gallantry under fire during a covert operation conducted while he was with the ISI. I was proud of him.

For much of his career we lived in cantonments, or military bases, except the time he served in the ISI. During those years we lived in town; he wore civilian clothes, and he made it clear that we were never to reveal his identity to anyone. I was to tell people that he was a businessman and nothing more. He would often sneak into India on dangerous missions. By the discussions I overheard in our house, I knew that he and his team kept an eye on diplomats, missionaries, and foreigners. I also knew which of the "diplomats" in the U.S. embassy worked for the CIA and which of the many American humanitarian workers in the country reported to them. We had strange "uncles" who visited us, and there was a lot of cloak-and-dagger activity around our house. I lived in a home where everything was hush-hush.

I grew up with the military and came to love the uniforms, the soul-stirring skirl of bagpipes, and even the sweet smell of burned cordite at the firing ranges. To this day, I have a passion for the musical wail of bagpipes. Bagpipes are the only musical instrument classified as an "instrument of war." The sound of the pipes does something to the heart of a soldier. For me, I can say that its effect has not diminished; it still causes my blood to warm and my eyes to tear.

As a little boy I grew up with the sight and sound of bands playing stirring marches like "Heilan Laddie," "Bonnie Dundee," "A Hundred Pipers," the slow march "Skye Boat Song," the incomparable lament "Flowers of the Forest," and other melodies so loved by the Scots. For over a century, on different battlefields in far-flung places, our regiments had served alongside and established strong bonds with Scottish Highland regiments. Through this long association our army had adopted the enduring traditions of bagpipes and tartan. As a child, I decided that one day I too would march to those pipes and drums wearing the khaki uniform my father wore with such pride.

My father rose to the rank of general, as did one uncle and three cousins. Until recently, two of my uncles and two cousins were cabinet ministers in the government, and my mother was a member of parliament. We socialized with the military elite and dignitaries from politics and business. Among our close friends was the late General Zia-ul-Haq who served as president of Pakistan until his aircraft was blown up in flight some years ago. One of my old classmates and friends was his aide-de-camp and died with the general.

The environment I grew up in was thoroughly Muslim, and I had no knowledge of Christianity or its doctrine.

In my early years, my father was not an overly religious man. I remember him facing Mecca and praying to Allah every evening, but then he and my mother would go to the army officers' club or some nightclub in the city, sometimes returning home late and intoxicated. We had sizable stocks of liquor at home, yet my parents often hosted all-night prayer and Quran recital meetings in our house. It was the way we lived, and I never thought of this as a double standard. It was the normal lifestyle for moderate Muslims. As the years went by, however, my father shifted from "moderate" to "fundamentalist" Muslim. He ceased drinking alcohol and grew more religious, even making a number of pilgrimages to Mecca. It was a sudden and stark change.

My mother was born in New Delhi, India. Her oldest brother was my father's best friend and classmate when they were cadets. It was through that friendship that my parents met. She came from a talented moderate Muslim family that was active in the performing arts. Her sister was a protégé of the famous Oscar-winning director Satyajit Ray and became a famous movie star in India. My mother also had talent. In those days, before the advent of television, everybody listened to radio. She was a well-known singer, and she also read the news. In addition to performing on radio, she received frequent invitations to sing at concerts and in musical soirees. She often organized musical gatherings at our home, and our musically talented friends would come, sing, and play their instruments through the night.

I have one younger brother. My father, ever the military man, named him Rommel, after Field Marshal Erwin Rommel, the World War II German general. An ardent anti-Nazi, Rommel was a gentleman soldier of the old school and one of the most brilliant commanders of all time. Had he been on the Allied side, history would hail him as the greatest general of the war. His exploits in the North African desert earned him the nickname the Desert Fox. My father admired Rommel so much that he named his second son after him.

My father engaged religious tutors who came to our home and taught me to read the Quran in the original Arabic. I memorized several chapters and verses from the Quran and could recite them verbatim, yet I could understand only bits and pieces of what I was reciting. Never having lived in the Middle East, I was not fluent in Arabic, yet my teachers made me read the Quran in the language. Muslims consider Arabic holy because it was Muhammad's mother tongue and the language in which the Quran was revealed. They believe there is special merit in reading the Quran in its original language. This is why many Muslims claim they have read the Quran but have never understood it. Having never learned classical Arabic, Muslims find the words they read meaningless. Only a small percentage of the world's Muslims can speak the language.

The environment I grew up in was thoroughly Muslim, and I had no knowledge of Christianity or its doctrine. I only knew that it was a religion started by the prophet *Isa*, as Jesus is known by Muslims. I, like every other Muslim, believed that Islam was the only path to God. I grew up with the words "There is no god but Allah, and Muhammad is his prophet" ringing in my ears.

> *People who have been touched by such demonic power soon become subject to spiritual oppression. . . . The power of God, on the other hand, brings restoration, healing, assurance, love, joy, and peace to the one touched by Him.*

We would visit the tombs of Muslim saints, where we would pray, asking for Allah's favor. My father leaned toward Muslim mysticism, especially the philosophies of Sufism. He was a devotee of a number of Muslim mystics. I accompanied him on his regular visits to see them. Some of these mystics were strange and said peculiar things. We held these men in awe and never thought of questioning their credibility. I concluded that what I took to be their strangeness were signs of their being close to Allah. After all, wasn't that what mysticism was all about?

I remember one such holy man with magical powers who visited our home. His name was Bahawal Shah, and he lived in a village outside the city of Sahiwal in the Punjab. He was believed to be 125 years old. My father had brought him in to pray for our family and to bless us. This was a great honor, as this man never left his village to go anywhere, yet the mystic agreed to come. The old man ordered a kerosene stove brought into the house. Servants brought the stove, placed it on the floor, and turned it on. A large wok-like pan of oil was set on the burner and allowed to heat until it boiled.

Then came the order.

I, as the eldest son, was to place my foot into the bubbling oil. It is difficult for the Western mind to understand, but I had no choice but to obey.

"Your foot," the mystic said, motioning to the pan.

The old man began chanting in Arabic.

My heart tumbled, and my stomach twisted into a knot. The smell of hot oil filled the room.

Again, the old mystic commanded me to put my foot in the oil. My father didn't object; he just watched in silence as I raised my bare foot.

Time slowed; every eye fixed on me.

To refuse would insult the mystic and embarrass my father. It would be a sign that we lacked faith and were unworthy of the old man's blessing.

One more time, I looked to my father for help and saw nothing.

"Put your foot in the oil, boy," the mystic ordered.

I plunged my foot into the scorching liquid. To my surprise it felt like lukewarm bathwater. There was no pain, no burning, and no damage to my foot.

I recall another holy man who visited our home. He broke a leaf from a creeping plant and swung his arm around. A moment later the leaf had been replaced by a large sugar crystal. This experience and others deepened our faith in the power of Allah and the work of his mystics.

Today my perspective is different. What I once saw as miracles worked by Muslim mystics I now see as witchcraft. In those days, such things held me in awe. One thing I understand now is that demonic powers are real, but the power of God is greater. Demonic power can be outwardly spectacular, but it never adds anything positive to a person's soul; in fact, people who have been touched by such demonic power soon become subject to spiritual oppression. Many develop serious physical or mental illnesses. The power of God, on the other hand, brings restoration, healing, assurance, love, joy, and peace to the one touched by Him.

Those were lessons I would learn later—at the moment, I believed it all.

Socially, we belonged to the upper classes. We had a staff of servants who waited on us day and night. We hosted parties, dinners, musical evenings, and all-night card parties at our home; in fact, our house was a social gathering place for military officers, friends, and relatives. We ate well, served by our own staff of cooks. Large, hot breakfasts and sumptuous multicourse lunches and dinners were normal fare, and all of it served by dedicated domestics.

I grew up speaking three languages: English with my father, Bengali with my mother, and Urdu with our servants. Some years later, a fourth language, Punjabi, came into our home through Punjabi-speaking servants who joined our domestic staff. These four languages were used every day in our family. Today, my repertoire of languages has grown to seven, plus a few more in which I can get by if I have to. Languages come easy to me, perhaps because of my childhood.

I went to the best schools, run by Irish Roman Catholic priests and nuns. There were a great many "convent schools" in the country, and most parents considered them the best academic choice for their children. I remember that over the blackboard in every classroom hung a cross with the figure of a man crucified upon it. He seemed to be looking at us from the cross. On the back wall hung a portrait of a man wearing a crown of thorns. Blood trickled from His brow, and His heart was purple in color. He looked at us with suffering, sorrowful eyes. During the years I went to those schools, nobody told me who that man was and why He hung on the cross. I was just a little boy, but I often wondered about this. However, I never dared to ask my teachers, and no one took the initiative to tell me.

My early childhood was happy, and I have wonderful memories of those days.

That would change.

In 1962, my parents divorced. It was an acrimonious separation. Since I was only eight years old and divorce was a rare thing in that culture, I could not understand what happened. I had never heard of such a thing. To this day, I do not know the reason my parents divorced.

The army stationed my father at Dhaka, which was at that time the capital of the province of East Pakistan. Everything seemed to go as usual until one day we went to see my mother off at the railway station. I remember that day well: the train leaving, my little brother and I standing on the platform waving good-bye to her as the train chugged from the station. My father said she was visiting her mother and that she would return in a few days.

We waved at a mother we expected to return soon.

She waved good-bye to her children forever.

She never returned.

> *I was beaten, called names, and cursed*
> *daily, and for little or no reason at all.*

Over time, I began to realize how much my father hated my mother. He would not allow my brother or me to see her or anyone from her family. His long friendship with my uncle, my mother's brother, was no more. My uncle and my father were majors in the same infantry division, but they never spoke. My uncle lived only a couple hundred yards away from us, but my father made it clear that we were never to see or speak to him. I saw my mother only twice in the next twenty-three years, and those meetings were done in secret. I saw her for a few minutes when I was nine years old, and once for two days when I was seventeen. My mother is still alive at the time of this writing, and I do visit her on occasion. My mother is a nice lady, but sadly there is none of the mother-son chemistry.

My father remarried soon after the divorce. My little brother, four years younger than me, and I were told that this lady was our "new mother." My stepmother turned out to be a cruel woman. She was pleasant in the beginning, but after some time she turned violent, frequently beating my brother and me. The violence grew in intensity and frequency. Soon it was a daily routine.

As days turned into months and those months into years, the physical and emotional torture increased. I was beaten, called names, and cursed daily, and for little or no reason at all. My step-mother was always nice when my father was present, but when he was away, she became a different woman, a horrible person. Her temper was enormous, and I remember how she would grit her teeth in rage until I could hear sounds like bones cracking.

One day, after enduring a beating for a minor issue that was not at my fault, I plucked up enough courage to tell my father what was happening behind his back. He exploded in rage.

"How dare you accuse your mother!" He slapped me across the face. Pain shot through my head and neck.

"It's true," I countered.

He hit me again, then again. "I'll teach you to lie to me."

The beating continued, and so did his curses.

That day I felt I had lost my father, too.

My life had dissolved into a nightmare.

I began to read books, losing myself in the beautiful world of fairy tales, which offered me an escape from my bitter reality. Those imaginary worlds became a place filled with love, solace, and comfort. I often cried myself to sleep.

As the years passed, life became unbearable, and I began to lose my desire to live. I became withdrawn, insecure, and morose.

My once beautiful childhood had been stolen.

Chapter 2

PAKISTAN AIR FORCE COLLEGE

⤸

I
N 1967, WHEN I turned thirteen, I applied for admission to
the Pakistan Air Force College. Located in Sargodha in
northern Pakistan, the Pakistan Air Force enrolled quali-
fied cadets while they were still young, oversaw their education,
trained them, and then turned them into fighter pilots. It was a
prestigious appointment, and only a handful of applicants out of
thousands made the cut each year.

I pinned my hopes on this appointment. The air force college
had much to offer a young man like me, but my primary reasons
were more basic: I was desperate to leave home. The constant
abuse, degrading insults, and unrelenting tension were taking
their toll on me.

The application was just the beginning. There were tests—weeks
of grueling academic, psychological, and medical tests. At the end
of each day I wondered if my performance had washed me out of
contention. The tension mounted with each passing day. Then the
news came. The school accepted me as a cadet. That year more than
ten thousand young men made the same application and endured
the same tests as I did, but only twenty-nine were selected.

For me, the air smelled of freedom.

The Pakistan Air Force College was a closed environment, located adjacent to the air base at Sargodha, the largest forward operational air base in the country. The campus was located close to the end of runway 06-24, and I soon became accustomed to the ear-splitting roar of various aircraft taking off and landing—an activity that went on day and night. Soon I could tell the difference between F-104s, MiG-19s, Mirage IIIs, F-86s, T-33s, T-37s, and other aircraft by just the sound of their engines.

We slept in barracks crowded with sixteen beds. It was a Spartan existence. The summers were hot, with temperatures rising to above 120 degrees Fahrenheit, and the winters were frosty, with the thermometer dropping near and at times below freezing. The dormitory had no heating or hot water. Showering in the winter has remained an unforgettable experience. As the cold water hit our bodies, we would sing and yell battle cries at the top of our lungs, partly as a show of bravado and partly to try to make the ice-cold water more bearable.

Life consisted of academics, drills, parades, inspections, sports, long-distance runs, and marches. Demanding physical exertions were part of our daily routine. There were many sports fields and open spaces on the campus. We played soccer, basketball, hockey, cricket, or other athletics every evening.

Discipline was harsh, and physical punishment came quickly for any lapse of discipline. Even small infractions brought down the wrath of our superiors. They called these punishment sessions "extra drills," and we carried out the punishment under the afternoon sun. We ran "at the double" carrying old, heavy .303 Lee-Enfield No.1 rifles raised above our heads. At other times, we did a set of calisthenics called "frog jumping." The exercise required us to squat and hop forward like a frog. I saw many of my fellow students pass out during these sessions.

For misbehavior in the classroom or for substandard academic performance, our instructors gave us "detentions." These they enforced on weekend evenings when we would normally watch movies at the open-air cinema. If placed on detention, we were forbidden to see the movies or participate in any of the other weekend activities.

I must confess that I was too familiar with both types of punishment. I was often up to mischief and found it difficult to stay out of trouble. For example, one night during detention a number of us asked for permission to go to the bathroom. It wasn't the bathroom that was on our minds. Instead, we went outside, picked up the little Fiat 600 belonging to the instructor on duty, lifted it over a hedge, and "parked" it in one of the nearby field hockey goals.

After the detention session was over, the instructor left and walked to where he had left his car. He was furious, certain that his vehicle had been stolen. He and the air force provost staff spent half the night looking for the vehicle but couldn't find it. Our instructor could do nothing but file a police report. The next morning, we marched to our morning parade, and there stood the car inside one of the goals of the hockey field next to the parade square—right where we left it. We got a good laugh, and no one ever suspected.

I aspired to be a fighter pilot in the Pakistan Air Force; we all did. Our heroes were fighter pilots, past graduates who often come to visit their old alma mater. They billeted in the officers' mess not far from our barracks.

I remember one pilot who visited us one evening. He was a flight lieutenant, and I considered him a role model. He had won the Sword of Honor for the best all-round cadet at his graduation from the Pakistan Air Force Academy in Risalpur. He had been a part of our squadron when he was at the college and was now with the No. 5 Squadron at Sargodha Air Base, flying the latest French-built Mirage III aircraft, the pride of the Pakistan Air Force. He was a regular visitor and often spent time with us. I remember one evening he sipped tea and relaxed with some of us. The image of

15

him in his flying overalls is still clear in my mind. He would be flying that evening, he told us.

The next morning we learned he had crashed and died. His Mirage III fighter had hit the ground as he executed a low flyby. The news of his death was sobering. Later I would see the flag-draped coffin that held his remains. I stood at attention and saluted. The incident jarred everybody and reminded me of the frailty of human life. I came to understand that we are all only a heartbeat away from eternity.

> *I began to take long walks in the dark, weeping and asking God why He had created me. I hated myself, and I cursed the day I was born.*

Each day started with a parade, inspection, and a reading from the Quran. Indoctrination in Islam was a regular part of our training. Fasting during the month of Ramadan was compulsory. I found the fasting interesting. We would start the fast at 3:00 a.m. every morning, with a huge meal consisting of fruit, eggs, yogurt, bread, butter, meat, and other delicacies. We then fasted the whole day until just after sunset, all the while working in the heat of the day without letting a drop of water touch our lips. The fast was so strict that even swallowing our own saliva would break the fast.

We finished the fast at sunset with evening prayers, and then we stuffed ourselves on a feast of dates, fruits, meat, bread, lentils, and desserts. This month of fasting was supposed to purify us spiritually, and we avoided swearing, cursing, lying, and telling dirty jokes during the holy month. At the end, however, we reverted back to our old ways and remained the same sinners that we had always been. The fast, I learned, brought no lasting change in our nature.

Friday prayers in the mosque were also compulsory. Some of

the cadets were more religious than others and prayed five times a day—every day.

I had thought that getting away from my father and step-mother would solve my problems. I was wrong. The beatings, the emotional and physical torture that I had endured since the age of eight, had left open emotional wounds. No matter how hard I tried, the past followed me like my shadow. I had deep-rooted problems. These problems affected my academics and overall per-formance so much that my superiors sent me to a psychologist for tests and evaluation.

Although the doctors found me normal, they were at a loss to explain why I was at the bottom of my class. I couldn't focus on my reading, couldn't concentrate in class, and was often lost in a world of my imaginations, fantasies, and daydreams. I began to take long walks in the dark, weeping and asking God why He had created me. I hated myself, and I cursed the day I was born. Some ill-defined anchor was dragging me into the dark abyss of despair.

My first major challenge was the high school examinations. These were administered, not by the air force college, but nation-ally by the Board of Education. In that part of the world, children start their schooling at a much younger age than in the West, and I had recently turned sixteen. It was now time for the national high school exams, and it was important that I do well.

Having a few days off, I decided to visit my father, who was com-manding a brigade in Lahore about 150 miles away. On the last day of my leave, he drove me to the railway station where I would take the train back to Sargodha. We passed the time talking, first about little things, then he changed subjects.

I had tried desperately to be found worthy of my father's love but always fell short— always.

I shifted in my seat. My father was staring at me, his eyes hard as flint. His mouth lowered at the corners, then stretched to a tight line. I knew the small talk was over.

"All these years…" He shook his head as if he were looking at trash that someone had discarded. "I've given you everything, and still you are a disgrace."

Something burned in my stomach. "I'm trying to do my best, Father—"

"You're worthless. You're worthless to me and to everyone. It's hard to call you son." He looked away. "The only reason you remain my son is because it is legally so."

I opened my mouth to speak, but whatever words I had, had been engulfed in the burning sorrow that surged in my heart. His words landed hard, and I thought I felt something breaking inside.

"Before you get on that train, know this," he said, "I will disown you if you do not do well on your exams. Do you hear me? Disown you. If you fail, you will dishonor me and disgrace the family. I will not tolerate you damaging my good name."

There was nothing to say—no argument to make. Rebuttal was useless. All I could do was hope the train would arrive early.

The shock and pain were enormous; each comment pierced me like a scalpel. I cried all the way back to Sargodha. I had tried desperately to be found worthy of my father's love but always fell short—always.

His cutting remarks turned up the heat on the cauldron of emotion boiling within me. Sorrow raged for a time, but soon it was replaced with determination.

I'll show him, I said to myself. *I'll show him that I am as good as anyone else.*

If I could do well on the tests, then he would have to be proud of me, and our relationship would be restored. Maybe, just maybe, things would return to the happy days of my early childhood.

I threw myself into my studies like a man possessed. I worked as hard as a youth my age could. Nothing else mattered. Then the exams came.

I still do not understand how I did it, but I passed with excellent grades. Not only did I do well, but I was also one of the top three hundred fifty students in the national exam group, a group consisting of tens of thousands of students.

I felt relief and a powerful sense of accomplishment. I had set out to make a difference; I had done everything I could to earn my father's approval. My father, however, gave no sign of appreciation. The only word I received was how the son of a friend had done better. He was still ashamed of me. It was clear now: no matter how hard I tried, I would never be good enough.

Why even try? I asked myself. *No matter what I do, it will never be enough.*

My father may not have been impressed, but others were. Some saw my good grades as a miraculous act, a sign that Allah could perform wonders.

Despite their praise, I was discouraged that my efforts failed to win my father's affection. I stopped trying and soon fell again to the bottom of my class. No one encouraged me. In my eyes, I was a born loser, a complete failure, and soon I felt that I had no reason to live. My grades declined so much that one of my instructors wrote on my annual report, "He is hopeless. Only Allah can help him."

I couldn't disagree.

Chapter 3

WARS WITHIN AND WITHOUT

N 1971, TROUBLE started brewing in the eastern province of Pakistan, now called Bangladesh. Tensions mounted daily, and soon the Bengali people rose in a mass movement for freedom. Their goal was independence from Pakistan, and they were determined to have it.

Pakistan came out of old British India. The British ruled India for a couple of centuries, and in the early 1900s, an Indian movement for independence arose against the British Crown. To complicate matters, the Muslims of India were wary that the Hindu majority would treat them unfairly after India became independent. The Muslims, as a result, formed a separate national state from India and called it Pakistan.

In 1947, before the British left, there were referendums held in every state, province, and kingdom in India to determine whether the local citizens would choose to be part of either Pakistan or India. Areas with a majority of the Muslims joined Pakistan, while those with non-Muslim majorities chose the new Republic of India. On August 14, 1947, when the British left, Pakistan was born as an Islamic state. The next day, India became a secular state.

In 1971 the Muslim majority areas in the western parts of British India joined together to form West Pakistan, while the Muslim majority province of East Bengal at the eastern end of British India became East Pakistan. Because of this Pakistan was a geographical oddity, with two provinces separated by the fifteen-hundred-mile-wide mass of India.

The two provinces were vastly different from each other. It was a mismatch from the beginning, a marriage doomed to fail. West Pakistan was almost six times larger in area than East Pakistan, but East Pakistan had many more people. West Pakistanis were Baluchis, Sindhis, Pathans, and Punjabis. East Pakistanis were Bengalis. They spoke different languages, and their ethnicities and cultures were vastly dissimilar. Even the way they practiced Islam was different.

The West Pakistanis, though the minority, dominated the government. In point of fact, it was the inhabitants of the Punjab province who were the dominant force in the military and thus ended up controlling the government (although most of the founding fathers of Pakistan were non-Punjabi).

> *When the news of the atrocities came out, I was overwhelmed with shame—I had worn the same uniform as those murderers.*

The Bengali of East Pakistan felt the Punjabis looked down upon them, that they were objects of constant discrimination. In 1970, after years of military dictatorship, Pakistan had its first-ever national democratic election. East Pakistan's ethnic political party won the majority of seats at the elections, and the Bengalis rejoiced. They were eager after all these years to have their say in running the country.

The West Pakistani–run military government responded

immediately to the East Pakistani victory by annulling the election and imposing martial law upon East Pakistan. The Bengalis, realizing that their dreams would remain unfulfilled as long as they were tied to West Pakistan, rose in a movement for liberty and self-determination. They wanted their province to secede and become an independent nation—Bangladesh, meaning "the land of the people of Bengal." There were strikes and huge protest rallies all over East Pakistan, and the federal government responded with a mass deployment of troops in the province. More than ninety thousand troops invaded by means of massive sealifts and airlifts. Arriving in East Pakistan, the troops systematically and brutally butchered the Bengalis. Thousands died.

The Punjabi troops of the Pakistan army worked in a gruesome, methodical way, targeting doctors, professors, teachers, students, and anyone who possessed leadership skills and slaughtering them.

The Pakistan army also disarmed all ethnic Bengali military servicemen and massacred many of them as they slept in their barracks. They also killed the men's wives and children. Ironically, many of the victims had in earlier conflicts fought valiantly for Pakistan.

The Pakistan army rampaged through the countryside, murdering Hindus and Bengali men of military age.

Three of my cousins who lived in East Pakistan were pulled from their home and forced to line up with other young men and boys. It was clear they were moments from death. The officer who led the army detachment raised his gun and shot one of the Hindu boys in the head, and then fired two more rounds into him as his body lay trembling on the ground. My aunt who was hiding in a nearby house went out of her mind with grief when she heard the shots. She assumed those gunshots had killed her three sons.

Then the major aimed his pistol at my cousins. That was when one of them had the presence of mind to blurt out my father's name. The officer knew of my father and lowered his gun. He released them, and they wasted no time leaving. Imagine my aunt's relief when the boys returned home safely.

The sad thing is that the government had imposed such effective curbs upon the media that we who lived in West Pakistan knew nothing of the atrocities committed by our army. Had we known how they had disgraced the honor of our colors and our uniforms, we would have felt great shame. For years the horrors were kept from the people of Pakistan.

When the news of the atrocities came out, I was overwhelmed with shame—I had worn the same uniform as those murderers. For years, I refused to wear my uniform or medals to special occasions because of the disgrace. In later years, however, I began to wear my medals and beret at veterans' functions, because I realized my old regiment had fought with honor.

We inherited our military tradition from the British, and as such we who serve take a personal pride in our parent regiments. The regiment is like a family, and my regiment never committed atrocities, nor did we ever turn our guns on civilians. We even treated the prisoners we captured in an honorable manner. To this day, I refuse to honor soldiers of any army who dishonored themselves by violating the Geneva Convention by killing unarmed civilians or by shedding innocent blood. Such acts are unjustifiable and indefensible.

The mayhem and destruction led to an exodus of refugees. Hundreds of thousands of people fled East Pakistan seeking safety and refuge in neighboring India. This included many servicemen and able-bodied young college students who managed to survive the killings. Once safely across the border into India, these men formed the Bangladesh Liberation Army. They then crossed the border back into East Pakistan and engaged the Pakistani army in guerilla warfare. While my father, some cousins, one uncle, and I wore the Pakistani uniform, another one of my uncles and several cousins were part of the opposing liberation forces. One of my uncles was an officer in the liberation forces and became a hero.

He received the highest decoration for valor under fire. He lost an eye in that terrible war.

Because India helped the Bengali liberation movement, tensions rose between India and Pakistan. Both sides deployed troops all along the border, and war with India was just a matter of time.

In some ways, the war was symbolic of what I was feeling. As battles raged on the ground and in the air, a long-standing war in my soul had grown more intense. Despair was my constant companion. I no longer wanted to live. Thoughts of suicide echoed in my mind. Not a day passed that I didn't consider taking my own life.

Only one thing stopped me: I had a keen awareness that I was a sinner and feared I would go straight to hell if I died. Heaven and hell were realities to me, and my fear of eternal torment kept me alive.

The fervor of jihad consumed the whole nation, and I joined the rising tide of Muslim fanaticism.

In my mind, there was only one way out of my predicament.

I learned, as every Muslim does, that dying in a holy war, or jihad, meant a straight admission into heaven. Knowing any war against India was always a holy war, I began to prepare myself for jihad and martyrdom. I did this by plunging headlong into radical Islam.

The fervor of jihad consumed the whole nation, and I joined the rising tide of Muslim fanaticism. I spent more and more time fasting, praying, and reading the Quran at the air force mosque. My zeal became obvious, and our religious leader entrusted me with announcing the summons to prayer from the minaret of the mosque.

I wept before Allah, pleading with him to grant me martyrdom in the coming war against India. If Allah answered my prayers, then I would soon be in heaven. There was nothing more important to me.

The tension at the India-Pakistan borders grew. Religious and nationalistic fervor swept up the nation in frenzied fanaticism. Posters, billboards, bumper stickers, and newspaper advertisements proclaimed, "CRUSH INDIA." By then, a few skirmishes were taking place at the border between forward elements of Indian and Pakistani troops. These minor skirmishes escalated into battles with infantry and artillery involved. The skies over Kashmir saw dogfights as opposing air forces tried to dominate one another.

I knew full-scale war was imminent. At Sargodha, we worked hard at the air base, digging trenches, filling sandbags, constructing bunkers, and building up ground defenses. Sargodha was Pakistan's main forward air base, just a few minutes flying time away from India, and there was always a flight of fueled and armed fighter craft on standby at the end of the runway, ready to scramble the moment the alarm sounded. Ten miles away, stationed on a two-thousand-foot-high mountain, was a powerful radar station that constantly scoured the skies for enemy aircraft. We were preparing for war.

Once the base was ready, my fellow cadets received assignments to various places. I went to Lahore, where my father commanded the divisional artillery brigade of the famous "Tenacious" 10th Infantry Division, a formation that had fought against the Germans in North Africa during World War II.

Skirmishes became war when hostilities erupted on December 3, 1971. I tried desperately to join the battle at the front lines and die, but I lacked the proper infantry training. My commanders refused to let me go. I did other duties in the rear and looked for opportunities to get into the action. It finally came when I heard about and volunteered for an especially hazardous ground-defense mission called Operation Kite Shooting.

The Indian air force had begun a daily attack on the three bridges that spanned the Ravi River, west of Lahore. These bridges were lifelines between the city and the rest of the country. If the Indian army destroyed those bridges, they would cut Lahore off from the rest of the country, thus making it easier for troops to overtake the city. Lahore, one of Pakistan's largest cities, was less than twenty miles from the India-Pakistan border. The loss of Lahore would bring Pakistan to her knees.

Indian aircraft attacked these heavily defended bridges several times daily but could never hit them. The Pakistan army's anti-aircraft defenses were superb, and every day I watched Indian aircraft going down in flames. In the face of repeated failure, the enemy air force changed tactics. They flew in at treetop level, flying over the almost dry riverbed of the Ravi. They came close to destroying one of the bridges.

Operation Kite Shooting was our effort to protect those vital structures. Several all-volunteer, two-man teams with MG1A3 machine guns—each delivering a blistering eighteen hundred rounds per minute—were dug in the sand of the riverbed and lay in wait for the enemy aircraft to make another pass.

The next time Indian aircraft came to make their bombing run on the bridges we hit them with an unpleasant surprise. We opened up with all our firepower, sending streams of concentrated tracer fire into the sky, hitting the enemy craft. They flew off trailing smoke. Operation Kite Shooting was a resounding success.

It was hazardous duty for us. Our kite shooting teams were set upon and strafed by the aircraft. One officer I knew escaped death by the skin of his teeth after a 30 mm cannon round cut through the right shoulder epaulet on his uniform. He trembled with fear for days and at times could not even speak, so close he had been to death.

More effective defenses replaced the Operation Kite Shooting maneuver. This included the deployment of 12.7 mm quads and 37 mm LAA guns at the place we had been. I was no longer needed at Operation Kite Shooting.

After that, the closest I got to the battle was at the artillery command post, where I served as an intelligence officer. In the distance I could see the muzzle flashes of the big 155 mm guns lighting up the cold December night as they engaged enemy positions. I could hear the sounds of the battle raging not so far away and did my best to get into the thick of it, but it just didn't work. I was, however, to see action later on in 1972, up in the mountains of Kashmir.

Low-level air raids were an everyday occurrence. When the enemy aircraft came in, they attacked not only their targets but also any source of anti-aircraft fire. With this in mind, I got on a rooftop with a rifle during an air raid to open fire on enemy aircraft. Everybody was so terrified that they dragged me off the roof. They thought I was a madman, but I had a death wish. I wanted so desperately to die, because martyrdom in a "holy war" would open the doors of heaven for me.

I was seventeen years old, and my greatest and unrelenting desire was to die.

The war, bloody and furious, lasted only a few weeks. Outnumbered and surrounded by the overwhelming numerical superiority of the Indian army, the Pakistani forces in East Pakistan fought until overwhelmed. They surrendered. Indian troops and liberation forces entered Dacca in triumph. East Pakistan became the independent nation of Bangladesh. The United Nations then stepped in and negotiated a cease-fire in West Pakistan.

Thousands of young men died, and the battle left large numbers maimed or crippled for life. I visited the military hospital, overflowing with battlefield casualties. The things that I saw would turn the stomachs of the most hardened.

I saw the realities of war.... It is horrible, meaningless, and degrading. It is man at his very worst.

My friends had not been exempt. They suffered like all the rest. I remember an infantry lieutenant from the Baluch Regiment, fresh out of the School of Infantry and Tactics. His jeep ran over an antitank mine as he was on his way to join his battalion. The explosion removed half of his foot. His driver died immediately.

Another lieutenant of the Punjab Regiment, a Bengali, had half his leg blown off by an antipersonnel mine as he led his platoon on an attack across a minefield. Disregarding his pain, he rose on his remaining leg, using his rifle as a crutch, and continued the charge, urging his men forward. He struggled forward bravely until he fell again. His men, inspired by his bravery, rose and surged forward despite withering machine-gun fire and took the enemy position. This brave officer later lay in his hospital bed, screaming and moaning in pain day and night. Tears came to my eyes when I sat by his bed, held his hand, and tried to comfort him.

Yet another officer of the Baluch Regiment was fortunate. He had led his company into battle with steely courage and occupied an enemy position after a pitched battle against an entire Indian battalion. A whole enemy brigade, supported by armor and artillery, then counterattacked his position. A 7.62 mm round entered through his mouth, shattering his front teeth and passing through his neck, narrowly missing his spine. The Indian forces overran his company and wiped them out in a massive counterattack.

Many of his men had been shell-shocked and drowned in the knee-deep, icy-cold waters of the Sutlej River as they were retreating. I remember when this happened because I was at the artillery command post during the battle and heard it all over the radio. I recall his anguished pleas for artillery fire support during the crushing enemy attack, but it had not helped. The enemy was

29

unbreakable—unstoppable. After the company had withdrawn and the large enemy force had occupied the position and were digging in, my father ordered down such a heavy and concentrated artillery barrage upon them that the enemy troops and armor were decimated. I was at the artillery command post when it had happened, following the radio communications during the battle, and had seen the massive artillery barrage that followed.

I saw the realities of war. They were brands on my brain and only contributed to my despair. Later, I would see action in Kashmir. I saw men maimed, dying. It is easy to say, "I saw combat," but it is horrible, meaningless, and degrading. It is man at his very worst.

War may be necessary at times, such as when one country attacks another, but war in and of itself is evil. It is the consequence of man's sin, arrogance, hatred, and greed. Countries should wage war with the utmost reluctance and only as a last resort. Those who have never experienced combat and watched young men die do not fully understand how evil war is. Christians should be against wars, killing, and bloodshed because Jesus showed us a better way. There is nothing glamorous about it. The glorified image of war shown in Hollywood movies bears no resemblance to the horrible realities of real military conflict.

The numerically vast Indian Army outnumbered and overran the Pakistan Army in East Pakistan. Pakistan thus lost the war. Ninety thousand of our men became prisoners of war in India, all captured at the surrender of East Pakistan to the Indian Army. One of my instructors from the air force college was among them. The whole nation was in utter shock. If Allah was with us, a Muslim nation, how could we lose a war to the unbelievers of India? My faith and confidence in Allah crumbled. It seemed as if all that I had so fanatically believed didn't amount to much in reality. I became a confused agnostic, no longer knowing what I believed.

My heart-wrenching roller-coaster ride continued.

Chapter 4

WITHOUT DIRECTION

THE YEAR 1972 marked the end of my five years at the Pakistan Air Force College. Prior to graduation, my class went through the Inter-Services Selection Board tests in the military cantonment of Kohat. Most of us passed the four intensive days of physical and psychological tests thrust upon us. If I passed the tests, they would clear me for two and a half years of training at the Pakistan Air Force Academy in Risalpur, after which I would be a full-fledged pilot in the Pakistan Air Force.

But I was still disillusioned, hurt, and confused. Despondency haunted me. I had no motivation. As a result, I passed the Inter-Services Selection Board tests but failed the civilian exams at the end of the year. Most of my classmates went on to the Pakistan Air Force Academy, while others who were no longer medically fit to become fighter pilots joined the army's Pakistan Military Academy. I, by certain turns of events, received a commission as an officer with the Azad Kashmir Regular Forces and joined an infantry battalion in the mountains of Kashmir, one of the most beautiful places I have ever visited.

This was Leepa Valley, the closest thing to heaven that one

can find on earth. On clear nights, from a spot on a mountain we called 10046, I could see the lights of Srinagar (the capital of Kashmir) twinkling in the distance. It was beautiful, but this little piece of paradise saw bloodshed, too.

One of our companies, strengthened with a rifle company of Tochi Scouts, had dug in atop a mountain. It was peacetime with UN observers in the area. Although there had been no recent hostilities, the enemy wanted to dislodge our men from their location. They launched an unexpected, full-scale attack.

> *It dawned on me that what I was getting*
> *into was nothing short of madness.*
> *I had not stopped to think that what*
> *I was planning was terrorism.*

The Tochi Scouts were fiery Pathan tribesmen from the northwestern frontier tribes whose uniforms were tailored like their traditional dress. These were sons of the fearless tribesmen that the British were unable to subdue in their two-hundred-year rule over the region.

Our battalion, along with the Tochis, fought a pitched battle against a three-battalion-strong enemy force. The enemy, supported with heavy bombardment from their mountain batteries, attacked us again and again. Short on ammunition and rations, our battalion and the Tochis managed to hold our positions, defeating the enemy. Casualties were heavy on both sides, and our commanding officer, a friend and classmate of my father, died leading the battalion from the front. He was an incredibly brave, kind, and humble man, loved by those he commanded. He led by example and from the front. A round penetrated his helmet. He died like a warrior.

After I completed my service time there I left the battalion. Before I departed, I was offered by my fellow officers a captured enemy 9 mm Sten gun and HE-36 hand grenades to take as souvenirs. Like many soldiers, I took them.

I left Kashmir and the battalion and traveled to Lahore. I was now out of uniform, and I realized that I had no direction in life. I needed a cause to live for, something to consume me. The ninety thousand Pakistani servicemen who had surrendered in East Pakistan were still languishing in POW camps in India, and many young men my age felt that our government was doing nothing to bring them home. I wanted to do something about it. To fulfill this purpose, I conceived the idea of launching an organization that would strike Soviet targets. I was vehemently anticommunist, and I despised the Soviets because they had armed and supported India in the war against us. I wanted to make them hurt for choosing to side with India.

I decided to model the organization after the Palestinian Al Fatah movement; I would call it *Al Shamsheer*—"The Sword." I began to talk to my friends, trying to raise interest. I also needed weapons, ammunition, grenades, and explosives, so I began to talk to my contacts in the army, looking for ways to arm my group.

The organization was barely started, and I had only acquired one HE-36 hand grenade when a friend of mine, an army officer, came to see me. He was alarmed and made no secret of it. He warned me that military intelligence knew what I was up to and were planning to move against me if I went any further. He informed me that operatives of an army field intelligence unit had been eavesdropping on one of my phone calls to him—the call in which I asked him to procure some grenades for me. They then interrogated him. He got off the hook because he had not given me anything. As yet he had done nothing illegal.

My friend then pleaded with me to stop. It dawned on me that what I was getting into was nothing short of madness. I had not stopped to think that what I was planning was terrorism. This is one of the most morally indefensible things a man could do. Terrorists always kill innocent people.

I stopped immediately, and nothing further happened. Later I learned that military intelligence realized that this was just youthful foolishness, a passing flight of fancy, and they decided to let the matter rest. My record remained clean and unblemished.

As I look back at those days, I see the hand of God preventing me from becoming something evil and taking the lives of innocents. I am thankful to the Lord that I did not fall far into the madness that has possessed the minds of so many young people from my part of the world. Such violent thinking is a curse, and only the gospel of Jesus can break that curse.

I tried out different things in civilian life but lacked a sense of direction. My only desire was to flee from everything. I wanted to try civilian life, but the adjustment was difficult. For a time, I worked as a copywriter/creative executive at an advertising agency. To fit in, I grew my hair long, tried to talk hip, and wore the bright and flashy clothes so popular in the 1970s. I even bought a pair of platform shoes. Although I did well with the creative end of the work—creating film scripts, copy writing, creating slogans, visualizing ad campaigns, and more—I felt like a fish out of water. The lifestyle was foreign to me. Somehow girls, long hair, platform shoes, bell-bottomed trousers, and disco dancing were just not my thing. I was every inch a military type, and I just did not fit. So I quit and began to study to complete my college exams.

I decided to study intensively and finish a two-year course in six months. I chose military science as my major, something that I knew would be easy for me. In addition to two languages, I had to study subjects such as military history, the science of war, the art of warfare, the evolution of weapons and weapons systems, strategy and tactics, and other similar topics.

I was losing my grip on life itself. I knew that if I hit bottom, I would end my life.

After months of hard study I passed the exams at the top of my class. During this time I also served with a National Guard battalion. I was first in the different courses I took and was also the best marksman in the battalion. My picture was in the newspapers, and I even appeared on television leading a three-battalion-strong parade.

My life was an unsatisfying paradox. I excelled at things that didn't matter and failed at those things that did and were crucial to my future. It was a sad truth.

I grew more confused, and the confusion made my slippery slope all the more perilous. I slid into a life of sin and immorality. The despair was overwhelming, and I lived on the brink of suicide. Nothing I did eased the hatred I had for my life.

One day I received a letter from the army stating that they had selected me for a regular commission. I was enthusiastic because I could now make the military my lifelong career. When I went for some final tests, I was one of only four who passed the exams out of one hundred fifty candidates tested. Everything went well, and everyone felt that I should pursue the life of a career officer like my father, uncle, and cousins. The military, after all, was the only environment where I felt comfortable; it had always been a part of my life. I knew I would do well if I joined as a regular career officer.

It all made sense.

It was the wise thing to do.

It was my best opportunity.

I turned it down.

For some inexplicable reason, I began to have doubts about the whole thing. I didn't understand why, but something within me just would not allow me to sign the papers they sent me. It wasn't a case of indecisiveness but something deeper.

People began to think that I had gone mad. Turning my back on an opportunity as rare as this made no sense. But I could not bring myself to sign my name. Some unseen force seemed to be guiding my will in the matter and stopping me. I knew that if I signed up then, I would be in for a minimum of twenty-three years of service. Finally, giving no reason at all, I turned the offer down. In hindsight, I can see that it was the hand of God.

The military had been the only environment where I had felt good about myself, and I was walking away. My confusion grew, and my desire to run away swelled. I was losing my grip on life itself. I knew that if I hit bottom, I would end my life.

For a time, I worked at the Hotel Intercontinental in Lahore as a management trainee aiming for a career in hotel management. I liked the work. At the same time, I joined an evening training course to be a radio officer in the merchant marines. My idea was that by going to sea, making lots of money, getting away from it all, and leaving my roots behind, I would find the freedom and peace I so longed for.

I put my whole heart into it and soon was the fastest in my class in transmitting and receiving Morse code. The PMG exam for merchant marine radio officers was not far away, and my dream would soon come true. If that didn't work out, then I would stay with Intercontinental, a worldwide chain of top-notch hotels. I was working hard and felt that I could choose between either of these two careers and have a respectable life.

Hurt and rejection continued to eat at me. I had no real friends and was wary of people. I began to stutter when nervous, and I was nervous most of the time. Hatred toward my father, my stepmother, and my family was rotting my soul, and bitterness consumed me. With every new day, I felt that I lost a little more ground.

I wasn't the only one who felt life was not worth living. At a family gathering my younger brother Rommel attempted suicide.

The shrill screams of my stepmother shattered the still of the afternoon. Her screams soon degraded into vile accusations and razor-sharp curses—all aimed at my brother.

I raced to my brother's room and found him stretched out on the bed. He didn't move. All my stepmother's cursing could not rouse him. Saliva dribbled from the corner of his mouth. His face was ghostly pale.

> *As I stared at my unconscious brother, I knew why he did it and couldn't bring myself to be critical of him. He had only done what I had often wanted to do.*

For a moment, I stood mired in the concrete of shock, certain my brother was dead. One of the servants had the presence of mind to call for an ambulance. There was little I could do but wait and listen to my stepmother curse his unconscious form.

There had been a note, a message that made it clear that he could no longer take the beatings and abuse. His solution came from a bottle of sleeping pills.

The servant also called my father, who rushed home from brigade headquarters. Entering the room, he saw my brother's unconscious form and uttered not a word. He showed no sorrow, no remorse, no regret. He observed the scene with less emotion than a marble statue in a park.

That changed.

As the moments crawled by, he tensed and then went white as a sheet, seething in tight-lipped fury. Outsiders would now learn that our outwardly harmonious family was not as wonderful as it appeared. We had the kind of problems lesser families had.

I studied my unconscious brother and then looked at myself. We were a pair, both worthless and unloved. I was filled with deep sorrow. I missed my mother. I had not received a mother's love, having seen her only twice since the divorce.

I loved no one, and no one loved me. I was no longer certain how to receive love or how to give it. Memories of my lost childhood plagued me, and I couldn't set myself free of them in order to live a normal life.

I was twenty-one and had nothing to live for. As I stared at my unconscious brother, I knew why he did it and couldn't bring myself to be critical of him. He had only done what I had often wanted to do. For a moment, I envied him.

Fortunately, though, he was rushed to the hospital and his life was saved.

Chapter 5

STRANGE ENCOUNTERS

∽

NOT LONG AFTER, in December 1975, I was walking down the Mall, the main thoroughfare of Lahore. Thousands of people were on the streets, milling about, shopping, buying, and selling. My mind chewed on recent events: my brother's attempted suicide, my inability to settle on a career, and my constant feelings of inadequacy. The thoughts swirled in my mind, like bees around a hive, when I noticed a tall, white man in the crowd. His complexion and height made him stand out against the brown faces of my countrymen.

All I knew about Jesus Christ was that He was the prophet of the Christians and the founder of Christianity, just as Muslims had Muhammad, the prophet of Islam.

He had a broad smile, and as I approached I could see that he was handing sheets of paper to any who would take them. I studied the man for a moment and felt strangely drawn to him. He exuded a sense of peace, an inward peace, I did not have.

As I approached, he smiled at me and gave me some of the literature.

"Who are you?" I asked.

"I am a servant of Jesus Christ." He looked at me as if he could read my life as well as I could read one of the fliers in his hand. "I'm from England, and I travel all around the world telling people about Jesus Christ."

He said this as if such things were common on the streets of Pakistan. They're not. His words made no sense to me. All I knew about Jesus Christ was that He was the prophet of the Christians and the founder of Christianity, just as Muslims had Muhammad, the prophet of Islam. I also remembered reading in *Time* magazine about the new U.S. President Jimmy Carter having said, "I am born again." I didn't understand what that meant, but it seemed to have something to do with the Christian faith. I had never met a "born-again" person before. I had never met a preacher, nor had I ever been inside a church building. As a very young child in convent school, I had seen Catholic priests and nuns, but they had never told me about their faith.

I did not know this person, but there on that busy street something stirred within me. He spoke the name of "Jesus Christ," and something seemed to grip my heart.

I had never touched a Bible and did not have the foggiest notion what Christians believed. All I knew was that Christians existed, and that just as all Middle Easterners, Iranians, and Pakistanis were Muslims, all white people were Christians. As far as I knew, Adolf Hitler, Brigitte Bardot, James Bond, Mickey Mouse, and Marilyn Monroe were all Christians.

I left the smiling Englishman and continued on my way. But a hundred yards down the road I had an indescribable, irresistible urge to return to him. It's hard to explain, but it was as if a physical force kept me from taking another step. I felt compelled to go back to him. I returned to where he stood at the busy intersection of Hall Road, Beadon Road, and the Mall. I stood before him and found myself pouring out my heart. Without hesitation, I told this stranger all my hurts and longings.

He listened patiently, and when I had finished, he said, "Jesus can set you free."

Again, when he said "Jesus," something inexplicable seized me. The name was familiar yet strange. I had been taught that the prophet "Isa," as we Muslims called Jesus, lived and died thousands of years ago. Yet this man seemed to be saying that Jesus was real and alive and could turn my situation around.

"How can Jesus set me free?"

"It's simple. All you have to do is to ask Him to come into your heart."

Come into my heart? What does that mean?

All this was strange to me, but the talk of Jesus gripped my soul. There was something powerful in the name Jesus. Every time he uttered it, I felt something move within me.

I had tried everything else: various forms of Islam, agnosticism, worldly living. Why not give Jesus a chance?

"OK," I said. "I want to receive Jesus into my heart if He will help me."

The Englishman narrowed his eyes as if trying to look into my heart and judge my real intentions. A second later, he took me by the elbow and led me a few yards away. There, in front of a Bata shoe shop and a pharmacy, he said, "OK now, let's pray together. Bow your head, close your eyes, and say this prayer after me."

I did as he told me to and repeated the words of the short prayer.

"Jesus, come into my heart and set me free. Thank You, Jesus. Amen."

That was it. Nothing formal. Nothing flowery. Just a handful of sincere words.

I opened my eyes. I felt different. I couldn't tell what it was, but I suddenly felt strange inside. I felt lighter, as if a crane had lifted the burdens that had threatened to crush me. A little spring of living water had begun to bubble inside my soul. The feeling was and remains beyond words.

"What happens now?" I asked him. I stared into his smiling face.

"Let's meet at the YMCA tomorrow at 10:00 a.m."

"YMCA, 10:00 a.m.," I agreed.

A walk down the street had changed my destiny.

Returning home from this unexpected meeting, I felt odd—changed. My senses seemed sharper. What was it? Why did everything seem brighter? Why were colors brighter than before?

That evening a friend came over and suggested that we go out and "have a good time." "A good time" meant doing things best left unsaid on these pages. It was a natural suggestion. Tariq, a few others, and I used to walk the wild side together. This evening, however, I said no.

"What's wrong with you?" he asked. "Are you unwell?"

"Nothing is wrong, and I am well," I said, "but I can't do those things with you anymore. Something has happened to me. I feel different."

"What do you mean, different? You look the same to me." He looked disappointed.

"I have Jesus living in my heart." I let the words pour out without thinking about what I was saying.

The dirt was gone. Everything looked different. Life itself seemed worth living.

Tariq exploded into hysterics. "What? Do you mean you've become a...Christian?"

"I don't know. I don't think so. I don't know what Christians believe. All I know is that Jesus lives in my heart and that He has set me free."

Tariq looked at me the way a psychiatrist studies an insane

man, then he began to pace.

"You can't do this. We are Muslims!" He was shouting.

The next few minutes were filled with his heated words. He questioned my sanity. He reminded me of our Muslim faith (which, ironically, he was willing to set aside for a night on the town).

Finally, he left—but he wasn't done with me.

He went home and wrote a long letter to my father stationed in Multan, a city about six hours driving distance to the south. In the letter he told my father what I had done and that it would be best if he would come to Lahore immediately. Clearly his son had lost his mind. How else could he explain all this new talking about Jesus Christ?

Tariq's negative confrontation did not lessen the fire that burned within me. I had my own night on the town, walking the streets praising Jesus for the first time in my life. The love of Jesus gripped me and filled my soul to overflowing. I had never experienced such love, such warmth, and I could not stop worshiping Christ. I remember walking on the streets and loudly singing again and again a famous song that I had heard a thousand times, "Your face is always before my eyes wherever I go; what else can I but do if your love holds my heart in its grip?"

The words had a new meaning to me, and I was giving new meaning to them. Great peace had filled my being. I felt as if I had been washed and scoured on the inside. The dirt was gone. Everything looked different. Life itself seemed worth living. I had found a wonderful Savior. I did not yet understand the fullness of what He had done for me. I did not know about His death on the cross for me. All I knew was that He had come into my heart. He had set me free, given me peace and joy, and I felt like a new man.

I walked until late that night, singing to Jesus songs of worship and praise, songs that I made up as I walked. Wave after wave of praise and worship poured out of the depths of my being to this wonderful Jesus.

For the first time in years, I didn't want to die.

I went to the YMCA at ten o'clock the next morning to keep my appointment with the Englishman. He wasn't there, so I waited. In fact, I waited all day, but he never turned up. I went again the next morning and waited the whole day, but still no Englishman. I was so eager to know more about Jesus that I went back a third day to the same result. During those three days, I had undergone an amazing transformation. There was no doubt that I had been changed within; I had been made into a new person.

As I waited for the Englishman the third day, I saw a young man and woman enter. They sat down and took out some literature and began to sort. I noticed that it was the same kind of literature that the man on the street had given me. I approached them and asked about the Englishman. They told me that he had to leave the country suddenly because of an emergency.*

I told them about my encounter with him on the street, that I had received Jesus Christ and wanted to know more. The young man, a tall American named Judd McKendry, asked me to sit on a chair next to him.

He looked at me with his piercing blue eyes. "So you have asked Jesus into your heart?"

"Yes."

"Do you know the conditions that you have to meet if you want to follow Jesus?" he asked.

"No, I did not know that there were any conditions." It seemed an odd question.

---

* I never met the Englishman again. Years later I did some detective work and discovered that his name was Keith Frampton, the son of Mr. K. P. Frampton of Bromley, England. Mr. Frampton was a prominent Christian businessman and philanthropist with a great heart for God. He loved the Lord with all his heart and was a great supporter of missionary endeavors. I had the privilege of staying at the Frampton home and enjoying their hospitality and fellowship shortly before Mr. Frampton's passing.

"Yes, there are. I'll show them to you."

There was a Bible on the table. He opened it and placed it in front of me. He pointed to a passage and asked me to read. This was the first time I had ever seen a Bible. I read the verses aloud.

> And he said to them all, If any man will come after me, let him deny himself, and take up his cross daily, and follow me. For whosoever will save his life shall lose it: but whosoever will lose his life for my sake, the same shall save it. For what is a man advantaged, if he gain the whole world, and lose himself, or be cast away?
>
> —LUKE 9:23–25

"Do you understand what this means?" he asked.

"It means that to follow Jesus I have to deny myself and sacrifice everything."

I saw it, and the words of Jesus struck me at the depths of my being. I understood. Jesus was calling me to leave everything, deny myself, follow Him, and even to die for Him.

"Do you know what it means to take up your cross daily?"

"No," I admitted.

"Jesus took up His cross only once," he explained, "and that was when He was going to die for us. If you want to follow Jesus, you have to take up your cross daily. In other words, you have to be ready to die for Him every single day. If you are not ready to die for Him, you are not fit to live for Him. With Jesus, it is all or nothing."

I saw it, and the words of Jesus struck me at the depths of my being. I understood. Jesus was calling me to leave everything, deny myself, follow Him, and even to die for Him. That was the price I had to pay if I wanted to be His follower.

"Are you willing to meet these conditions?" Judd asked.

"Yes, I am," I nodded. "I have nothing to live for anyway. I have nothing to lose but everything to gain. After what Jesus has done for me, I will follow Him. I will leave everything and go wherever He leads. I am ready to lay down my life for His sake."

"Good," he replied. "You can start now."

Minutes later I was on the streets with Judd, handing out tracts, telling people what little I knew about Jesus. All I knew was, "Jesus will set you free if you ask Him into your heart." If they asked any other questions, I would point to the American on the other side of the street and tell them to ask him.

The love of God enveloped me, and tears came to my eyes. I cried. I was embarrassed because I suddenly felt like a child instead of the tough guy I wanted people to believe I was.

It had been just three days since I received Jesus, but I could already tell that nothing would ever be the same for me.

As I was walking down the street that day handing out tracts, I heard a voice speak to me. I turned around to see who it was but saw no one. At first I was frightened. Then I knew that it was the voice of God speaking to me.

"This is what you shall do the rest of your life," He said. "I shall take you all around the world, and you shall tell people about Jesus."

Unforgettable words. For so long I struggled to find a reason to live and a path to follow; now God was handing it all to me in a single sentence. A bolt of electric excitement fired through me.

After we handed out the tracts, the young American took me

to a little Christian bookshop in the YMCA. He gave me a pocket New Testament and took me to his home for a meal. I found a whole group of these young followers of Jesus—singles, couples, and children. They told me that they were from a group called the Children of God. Today, unfortunately, they have degenerated into a cult that calls itself the Family, but in those days I saw nothing that made me doubt that they were anything other than genuine Christians with a burning zeal to win souls for Jesus.

As I sat alone in their living room, Judd's daughter Bianca walked up to me, hugged me, and picked up a guitar. She began to sing about Jesus. The love of God enveloped me, and tears came to my eyes. I cried. I was embarrassed because I suddenly felt like a child instead of the tough guy I wanted people to believe I was.

The walls I built around myself crumbled to dust and were no more. I felt vulnerable and exposed. It was as though the young girl with the big blue eyes saw right through me, that she could view the wounded and frightened child that I was behind the mask.

The group prayed for me and showered me with such love that it left me overwhelmed. They hardly knew me, and yet they drew me into their circle as if I were a member of the family. Never in my life had I received such love. I had come home at last.* That night I went to bed in tears. I wept for joy at the love the Christians had shown me. I woke up before dawn and couldn't wait for the day to break. I was eager and longing to be with the Christians again.

I was twenty-two, but I had become a child all over again.

---

* Years later I was preaching in a large church in Augusta, Georgia, in the United States. Judd was there with his family. They came up for prayer, and I immediately recognized Bianca who had sung for me that day. She had become a beautiful young lady. When I prayed for her, I was so overwhelmed that I hugged her and cried as I had cried that day so many years ago.

Chapter 6

PERSECUTION

⁓

MY FATHER, HAVING received Tariq's letter about my unusual behavior, flew in to Lahore. Over the years, he showed little care for me; now, all of a sudden, he appeared to be concerned. There were reasons for this.

Any Muslim leaving Islam to follow Jesus faces harsh consequences. According to Islamic law, such apostasy is punishable by death, and a Muslim who becomes a Christian should be executed. Because of this, very few Muslims confess their newfound faith publicly. This is why there are so many "secret" Christians in Muslim countries today.

> *For three days they grilled me, insulted and humiliated me, questioned me, and called me demeaning, hurtful names. They limited my sleep to weaken my resolve and to break me mentally.*

Muslims who turn to Christ are often murdered by their families. Few, like me, survive. Most have to make the ultimate sacrifice for Jesus of laying down their lives. The authorities look the other way when such murders take place. It is considered an "honor killing," an act of virtue to kill a "Kafir," an "infidel" or "apostate" person—even if that person was formerly called family.

When a Muslim turns to Jesus, his or her relatives see it as a disgrace. It is a stigma upon the name and the honor of the family. In the Muslim world, maintaining the family's pride and standing in the eyes of society is foremost and the duty of every family member. The family, therefore, will first try to get the new Christian to return to Islam. This is first done through offers of money and material things, and if that doesn't work, then through threats and intimidation. If all this fails, the only way of salvaging the family honor is to kill the new Christian.

My father was furious, and he made no effort to hide the fact. I had disgraced him and the name of the family. He was duty bound to get me to return to Islam.

He gathered some of his military friends: a major general, a lieutenant colonel, and a major. For three days they grilled me, insulted and humiliated me, questioned me, and called me demeaning, hurtful names. They limited my sleep to weaken my resolve and to break me mentally. Everything about my life was brought into question. The words still echo in my mind.

"Who do you think you are? Who are you to talk about God and Jesus? You're evil."

"What's so special about you? You're useless... worthless."

"What happened to you that you've become so fixated with Jesus?"

They did acknowledge a change in me, that I was somehow different. That change, however, they attributed to bizarre reasons.

"Someone has hypnotized you. You're not thinking your own mind."

"You're under a spell."

And finally, "You've lost your mind. Your sanity is gone."

Day after day, hour after hour, late into the night, they hammered at me. They were relentless. Nonetheless, I felt great peace in my heart and took it all in stride. This angered them even more. After three days of interrogation and war for my soul, they finally concluded that I had been hypnotized or put under a magical spell. It was either that or I had lost my mind. Either way, their conclusion opened the door for their next action—my being admitted to a mental institution.

They took me for observation and evaluation to the psychiatric ward of the Combined Military Hospital in Lahore. I had never seen a mental institution before and was stunned by my first sight of the place. It was like a huge cage with a roof, locked from the outside and guarded by uniformed soldiers. The guards carried staves for protection. Only a portion of the rooms had walls; the rest of the space was marked off by iron bars. The place resembled a zoo. It is degrading to cage humans like animals.

> *The breathtaking presence of God filled my room, and I thanked Him for His goodness to me in spite of the adversity I was experiencing.*

Some of the poor souls locked in there were truly mentally ill; others were there for ridiculous reasons. One enlisted man was there for refusing to salute a general. He had done this because he was tired of the army and wanted out, but they had concluded instead that he was mad. Another was one of the thousands of beggars, mendicants, and the insane who roam the streets of Pakistan's cities. But this beggar was suspected of being a secret agent for Indian intelligence. Being a beggar was his disguise. This may sound strange, but such situations are normal for Pakistan. The country has harbored a national paranoia about India. Indian spies are supposedly running around everywhere, and the hordes of street people that roam the streets of Pakistani cities are always the prime suspects. Another inmate, a Pakistan Air Force sergeant, was there because he ceased believing in the existence of Allah and considered himself an atheist.

The gate closed behind me, and I found myself in a world I couldn't imagine. The doctors gave me five different kinds of pills to take three times a day. The medications were strong and made me dizzy. They were meant to sedate me.

I had smuggled in my pocket New Testament, but I could read no more than two or three verses at a time before the words would blur. The dizziness made it impossible to focus. I read small portions at a time. The Word of God strengthened and sustained me.

I spent my first Christmas as a Christian in that psychiatric hospital. Not having been born in a Christian environment, I knew nothing about Christmas except that it was the birthday of our Lord Jesus. So I decided to celebrate the Lord's birthday in a fitting way. I had a little cupcake given to me as dessert with dinner, and with it I had a little birthday party. I did not know any Christian songs, so I just read a few verses from the Bible and prayed. I remember how the breathtaking presence of God filled my room, and I thanked Him for His goodness to me in spite of the adversity I was experiencing.

During my two weeks in the place I managed to lead two people to the Lord Jesus: one was the atheist air force sergeant, and the other was a male psychiatric nurse, an Army Medical Corps sergeant who was assigned to watch over us.

One day he took me out of the "cage" into the hospital garden and said, "I have been watching you. There is nothing wrong with you, so why are you here?"

I then proceeded to share with him about my life struggles, my providential encounter with the Englishman, my simple prayer, and what Jesus had done for me. After some discussion, he told me he wanted the same experience with Jesus. We prayed, and there in the garden of the mental hospital, he received Christ as his Lord and Savior.

The medical officer in charge of the psychiatric ward, a captain, made daily rounds to check on the patients. He would talk to each patient and ask him or her questions to check on their condition. We were required to line up in our pajamas and stand at attention as he went down the line. The air force sergeant, confined there because of his atheistic views, was asked the same question every day, "Do you believe in Allah?" The answer always was, "No, there is no God." The psychiatrist would shake his head, mutter something to his assistant, who jotted something down in the man's file, then move on to the next man in line.

One day as the medical officer was on his rounds, the air force sergeant, who had now given his life to the Lord Jesus, announced, "I believe in Jesus Christ, and I am now a child of God."

The doctor knew instantly that I was involved in this transformation and gave me a horrified look. He decided that he had had enough of me. He discharged me from the hospital, reporting that there was nothing wrong with me. He concluded I was perfectly sane. It might have been a conclusion of convenience for him, a way of getting rid of me, but we were both glad to part ways.

I can't help but see the irony in this. I was institutionalized because I confessed that I had become a Christian; I was released from that institution because someone else, someone I had led to the Lord, confessed the same thing. As the poet William Cowper said, "God works in mysterious ways."

The medical officer may have washed his hands of me, but my father hadn't. After my release, he took me to his current "holy man," his religious mentor and guide at the time. This man first tried to talk me into coming back to Islam. I declined. This normally mild-mannered holy man then flew into an infernal rage. He angrily denounced me and cast a curse on me.

More irony. Instead of anything happening to me, he died a few months later.

The power of Jesus is greater than the power of the devil.

When curses and mystics failed, my father took me to Multan, under arrest, and kept me under guard in his house. My father's home was surrounded by high walls and guarded by soldiers around the clock. Then an interesting incident took place.

We knew a particular holy man who boasted of many contacts with the spirit world. He was in constant communication with *jinns*—what westerners call genies and what the Bible identifies as evil spirits. He believed he could call on these spirits to work for him. He could invoke strong curses on people and move and influence events through the demons he associated with. He could make things appear and disappear, make blood appear in swabs of cotton wool, and so on.

This man lived in Mailsi, a town about fifty-five miles away, and had visited our house before. We had seen hair-raising manifestations of supernatural activity around him whenever he went into action. Once, for instance, he had come to us because my father suspected that his ex-mother-in-law had paid someone to put a curse upon him. The mystic prayed and recited incantations. He then, among other things, took my father's mattress, bed sheets, pillows, and blankets to a well where he threw them in. Everything dematerialized before it hit the water. The water level in this rather wide well was about thirty feet below the surface, and somewhere along those thirty feet, the mattress, sheets, and everything else had vanished into thin air.

My father hired the so-called holy man to work his powers on me. For several days and nights he was in the bedroom next to mine praying, reciting incantations, and other mumbo-jumbo. Finally, he called me in to speak with him. The Lord had given me great peace, and I felt no fear although I was wary of going into his room. I expected black magic to flash all around me, but when

I walked into his room and saw he looked normal, I knew there was nothing to be concerned about. He looked at me and said, "I believe you are doing the right thing. Follow the path that you have chosen."

I was stunned.

He continued, "I shall tell your father to leave you alone. I shall tell him that you are doing the right thing, and that if you are wrong, you will come back."

The power of Jesus is greater than the power of the devil. The Bible says that even the demons know who Jesus is, and they tremble. The mystic was powerless to change someone filled with Christ.

This was not what my father wanted to hear. He decided that this holy man had missed it this time and started to look around for other masters of evil spirits to come and tame me.

I decided by then that I had had enough of this, but being under house arrest made it difficult to do anything about it. I looked for opportunities to escape, and I finally managed to do so a few days later by evading the sentries guarding the house. I traveled by bus to Lahore to join the Christians through whom I had received the Lord Jesus. I carried only seven rupees, at that time equivalent to less than a dollar, a couple of changes of clothes, a toothbrush, a blanket, my New Testament, and a few other small possessions.

I arrived in Lahore that evening and made my way to the home of the Christians. As I entered the house, I walked right into a prayer meeting. They were on their knees. I remember their cries of, "Lord, give us one disciple for Jesus from this nation."

That was me.

The Christians welcomed me warmly as a brother. They looked at me as an answer to prayer. In the meantime, my father had set the police and the army looking for me. I had to stay a step ahead of them, so I slept in a different place every night to make it difficult for them to catch me. My first night was spent at a flea-infested hotel for hippies near the main railway station in Lahore

City. It was only fifty cents a night, and I woke up in the morning
with the red bumps of flea and bedbug bites all over my body.

> **"Be careful with this man. I know for a
> fact that he has assaulted women at the
> youth hostel."**

I spent my second night at the more comfortable YMCA. It was
a one-night stay. They tossed me out the next morning. This happened after I walked into the office of the YMCA manager and ran
into a man there that I had met back in 1973. This man, a slick
talker and a sharp dresser, used to frequent the youth hostel in
Lahore where his friend was the caretaker. Together they sexually
assaulted single, young Western women, backpackers who would
stay at the youth hostel. Their modus operandi was to first befriend
these lonely girls, then offer them soft drinks laced with some drug.
They would then rape them while the girls were unconscious.

They attempted this on a young lady from Minnesota. This
young lady was backpacking overland through Pakistan on her
way to a university in Malaysia. I had come to know her and had
protected her from these predators after they had tried to get
her to drink the drug-laced soda. She had to literally run from
the place without her things. I took her into my protection and
went to the youth hostel to recover the possessions that she had
left behind. The two men were angry with me and threatened
me. They had even gone to the police, filing a complaint against
me for something that they had made up. I had not seen them
since.

Now, as I walked into the manager's office, I saw the same man
and recognized him straightaway. He recognized me, too. He was
a friend of the manager, and for all I knew he was planning to do
the same thing to women here at the YMCA.

He became nervous when he saw me and said to the manager,

"Be careful with this man. I know for a fact that he has assaulted women at the youth hostel."

The manager ordered me to leave the premises immediately and never to return. He refused to listen to my defense.

I was hard pressed on every side in those days, yet the Lord strengthened me daily. One of the most comforting elements in my life was Psalm 27. It is a well-known passage to most Christians, but it was new to me. I read its words frequently:

> The LORD is my light and my salvation; whom shall I fear? the LORD is the strength of my life; of whom shall I be afraid?...One thing have I desired of the LORD, that will I seek after; that I may dwell in the house of the LORD all the days of my life, to behold the beauty of the LORD, and to inquire in his temple....When my father and my mother forsake me, then the LORD will take me up.
>
> —PSALM 27:1, 4, 10

These words were so relevant to my situation they seemed written just for me. I spent about a month living on the run in Lahore. During that time I read the Bible as often as I could, memorizing a verse a day. I also prayed and testified about Jesus daily.

It was during those weeks that I received the greatest revelation of my life. It happened as I was alone one day, reading my Bible. I was reading Isaiah: "For he shall grow up before him as a tender plant, and as a root out of a dry ground....He is despised and rejected of men" (Isa. 53:2–3).

The last part hooked my attention. Jesus identified Himself with me. I read more: "Surely he hath borne our griefs, and carried our sorrows....But he was wounded for our transgressions, he was bruised for our iniquities; the chastisement of our peace was upon him; and with his stripes we are healed" (vv. 4–5).

Suddenly the message of the cross struck home. I could see it. I saw the cross, the foundation and focus of the gospel of Jesus.

For the first time, I saw what Jesus had done for me. I understood how Jesus took upon His own self my sins and torments. He took my sin, my shame, my guilt, and my burdens upon Himself so that I could walk before God as a free man. I began to understand and, more importantly, to appreciate the horrible price He paid. I began to grasp how much it had cost Him to save me, a lost sinner. The act of setting me free by coming into my heart had cost Him everything.

All my life it had seemed that nobody understood my pain, but Jesus not only understood it, He also went through it and bore it upon Himself.... Jesus received me, embraced me, and made me His own.

It was a new truth to me, and one that landed hard on my soul. Contemplating the agonizing price Jesus paid for me made me weep, and I wept for a long time. The tears would not stop. The sobbing poured from me in waves. The image of Jesus wearing a crown of thorns, bruised, hanging on the cross flashed in my mind time and time again.

"For me...for me..."

Words were useless. No term existed to describe my gratitude and my sense of unworthiness. *For me.* I could not fathom the depth of such love. He took my place. There is knowledge that is perceived in the mind, and there is knowledge that rips through a person's soul. It was the latter that pressed me to my knees.

All my life it had seemed that nobody understood my pain, but Jesus not only understood it, He also went through it and bore it upon Himself, taking it all away. He took my sin and my pain. When family and friends rejected me, Jesus received me, embraced me, and made me His own.

The biblical revelation of the cross transformed my life from the inside out. I began to see the cross of Jesus as the central theme of the Word of God. Since that day the cross has been the main theme of my life and my ministry. The account of the Crucifixion continues to grip me. It stirs my soul like nothing else can. Of all the men of God I know, nobody can quite preach it like my friend and brother Reinhard Bonnke. Whenever I listen to him preach the simple and wonderful story of Jesus, I begin to cry.

After decades in ministry, the power of the cross has not been diluted.

Chapter 7

REACHING OUT

WITH THE AUTHORITIES still searching for me, staying in Lahore became increasingly difficult. To avoid capture, I moved south to Karachi and lived there as part of a colony of the Children of God. The Children of God insisted new members adopt new biblical names to use as aliases instead of their legal names. Some of their name choices were comical. For example, one man was called "Habakkuk 2:4" (2:4 being his surname). Two young ladies were called "Ruth the Truth" and "Miracle Moon-garden." A wheelchair-bound man called himself "Hananiah Ironside," after Hananiah in the Bible and the paraplegic police detective Ironside from the popular TV series by the same name. A Canadian named Nicholas chose to be called "Chronicles" because the "nicles" in "Chronicles" sounded somewhat like his real name Nicholas, but everybody just called him "Chron." We had Asher, Jair, Bani, Melzar, Jeremiah, Ezekiel, Belshazzar, and Mahershalalhashbaz.

**I was public about my faith because Jesus
was public about His death for me.**

I had a plethora of biblical names to choose from, but I chose "Isaias" because of the impact that the fifty-third chapter of Isaiah had on me. Though not as common a name as Peter or John, it did not seem quite as laughable as some of the other names that I had heard, and that is what I was known as from then on. Later I was forced to change it to Hosanna after a nationally known magazine interviewed me and printed my picture. After some time, I dumped Hosanna, upon realizing how ridiculous it sounded. It was like being called "Hallelujah."

My days were spent reading the Bible, memorizing Scripture, telling people about Jesus, and handing out tracts. Many Muslims were fascinated by the gospel message. They made professions of faith but wanted to remain "secret believers." They feared reprisal and death. One of these men was a well-known politician who used to come to us secretly just as Nicodemus came to see Jesus. Another was a leading movie producer whose wife was a famous actress. There were doctors, attorneys, wealthy businessmen, and famous people.

I have never understood this thing about "secret believers" in Muslim countries. From the Bible I learned that Christians were not to hide their light under a bushel. Our Lord Jesus died for us, so shouldn't we be willing to die for the gospel, if that is the price we have to pay for our testimony?

I was public about my faith because Jesus was public about His death for me. Verses like Revelation 12:11 spurred me on: "And they overcame him by the blood of the Lamb, and by the word of their testimony; and they loved not their lives unto the death."

Jesus said, "Whosoever therefore shall confess me before men, him will I confess also before my Father which is in heaven. But whosoever shall deny me before men, him will I also deny before my Father which is in heaven" (Matt. 10:32–33). I had no desire for confrontation, and since coming to Christ I no longer had a death wish, but I couldn't bring myself to pretend not to be what I was.

I relished being part of a team of people whose main goal in life was to share with people the life and hope offered by Jesus. Together with two other men, I pioneered a beach ministry among the drug-using hippies at Hawke's Bay beach on the Arabian Sea coast. There were hordes of them, smoking the cheap and readily available hashish, lying on the beach stoned and all but oblivious to their surroundings.

The three of us traveled out to Hawke's Bay from Karachi, riding on the roof of an overloaded bus. We shared the bus not only with fellow passengers but also with goats, sheep, and chickens.

Our first night we slept in sleeping bags on the beach and under a canopy of stars. I remember waking in the morning with a huge black dog sleeping across my legs. I was scared stiff. He was massive. I slid inch by slow inch out of my sleeping bag, afraid to wake the beast. I collected a few rocks and threw them at him, hoping to shoo him off. The stones failed to intimidate him. He jumped up and rushed at me. For a moment my heart stuttered and lungs refused to work, certain I was about to become the dog's breakfast. Instead of attacking, he stopped right in front of me, tongue hanging out and tail wagging. Fortunately for me, the dog just wanted to be friends. From that moment on he followed me everywhere.

We found and rented a rustic beach hut. It had no running water. I was the designated cook and prepared from scratch a three-course meal for about thirty people every evening—on a single kerosene burner. There was no electricity, so we used kerosene lanterns for light in the evening darkness. We had no money, so we prayed frequently and trusted God for everything. The three of us would go out and invite the hippies. After they gathered at our hut, we would sing for them, do a short skit or testimony, feed them my three-course meal, and then spend the rest of the evening talking to them about Jesus.

Faith was the key to our efforts. We often traveled without food or money, preaching and witnessing to anyone who would listen and making our homes in small tents set up in parks or grassy places. Such efforts helped me learn to trust God for my daily needs. I found this beneficial as I soon found myself in many situations where only a miracle could meet my needs. I am happy to say God always met every need in every situation. I never lacked for anything. God was and is faithful.

> *"You may be walking in faith, but if you are not walking in love, then you are sinning against your brother."*

I recall the first time I was sent out on faith. It happened when I had only been a Christian for a couple of months. My team leader told me to take Jonah, who had been a Christian for just two weeks, on such a faith trip. We were to go out for twenty-four hours with no money and share Christ with the people we met. We were to trust God for breakfast, lunch, dinner, and a place to sleep.

"But I am a baby Christian," I protested. "I cannot take responsibility for a new believer."

My team leader's response has stuck to my soul ever since. "Every Christian is a leader. You're a leader whether you like it or not. Those who come to Jesus after you will see you as an example. You may have been a Christian for only two months, but the one who receives Christ today will look up to you as someone who has been around longer and therefore knows more. You and I have no choice but to be an example of faith to others. You better accept this fact, because that is the way it is and the way it will always be."

Thoroughly admonished, I took Jonah and headed out the door. We walked the streets all day, testifying about Jesus to any who would listen, and God provided us with good food to eat through the kindness of a man with whom we had shared the gospel. By evening, I was tired and eager to find a place to sleep. Nothing presented itself.

"Let's find a Muslim mosque," I suggested. "Mosques are always open twenty-four hours, and there are mats on the floor we can sleep on."

To Jonah the suggestion was unthinkable. "I do not want to deny Christ by sleeping in a mosque."

I tried to explain that sleeping in a mosque did not amount to a denial of Christ, but he was not convinced. Realizing that I now had a small rebellion on my hands, I decided to take Jonah back to the team base, leave him there, and go on alone.

We knocked on the door of the base at about midnight. My sleepy-eyed team leader opened the door. "You were supposed to be back tomorrow. Now leave and believe God—" he began.

"Please, listen," I pleaded, and explained the whole situation to him, hoping that he would take Jonah off of my hands.

My leader listened and took me aside to talk to me. "More important than faith is love," he said. "You may have the faith to sleep in a mosque, but his conscience obviously cannot handle it. You by your insistence are causing your brother to stumble. You may be walking in faith, but if you are not walking in love, then you are sinning against your brother. The Bible says that if your eating meat causes a weaker brother to stumble, then you have sinned. Now go back and trust God for a place to sleep that Jonah's conscience can handle."

I left chastened, having learned yet another lesson. God did give us a place to sleep that night. We slept in a little tent in the middle of a traffic roundabout in the middle of the city. The next morning we went back to our base, our mission accomplished.

We visited schools and witnessed on the streets, handing out tracts and sharing our faith. Many received Christ, and we would have meetings at our base twice a week with songs, skits, and sharing. While working on the streets, we would at times run into Muslim fundamentalists who would start screaming and ranting at us. A crowd would gather, and the fanatics would get the crowd worked up, leading them in religious chants. At times things would get dangerous, and just as the situation would become explosive, we would leave, regroup in another place, and continue our ministry.

On one occasion a plainclothes petty officer from naval intelligence arrested me in broad daylight on a crowded street. He told me that they had been watching us for sometime, and they knew beyond doubt that we were spying for and were financed by the Israeli government. He took me for interrogation to an infamous police "torture house" that lay in the center of the city.

When we reached the facility, we stood outside for a moment waiting for a guard to open the heavy steel gate to the facility. I decided to try to bluff my way out of this situation. I looked him in the eye and told him that my father was an army general and that I was a reserve officer. If he were to touch a hair on my head, then he would regret it for years to come.

"Do you know my father?" I gave his name and included the fact that he was a general in the army.

"You...you're his son?" he stammered.

My tone turned cold. "Perhaps you also didn't know that I am an officer in the army reserves."

He paled.

I turned and faced him, my gaze boring into his eyes. "Let's be clear about one thing, petty officer. You had better think long and hard about what you do to me. I don't know what you are planning, but if you touch a single hair on my head, I'll make your life miserable for years to come. I can't even describe what my father will do to you. Do you understand?"

His mouth moved, but no words came out.

"I asked you a question, petty officer! Do you understand?"

"Um, yes, sir. Of course, sir. It was my mistake. You can go."

"Go?" I shot back. "You arrest me in public, accuse me of being an Israeli agent, disrespect me, and now you want me to walk away as if nothing has happened?" I moved a step closer. "You have not yet saluted me or apologized. I am not going. Just take me inside and try to do what you want, then you can watch what happens to you."

The moment I finished, he came to attention with a snap, saluted, and began to apologize profusely.

I told him, "Don't ever let me see your face again. If I ever see you, you will regret the day you were born. Is that understood?"

"Yes, sir," he replied. I turned and walked away. I never saw the man again.

It was a narrow escape and I thanked God for it, but I wasn't out of the woods yet. My father still had the army and the police after me, trying to trace my whereabouts.

Still, I was free. For the moment.

Chapter 8

A PRISONER FOR CHRIST

∽

*I*N FEBRUARY 1976, the police finally located me and came to my apartment one afternoon. They arrested four of my friends and me and took us away for questioning. We were kept for forty-eight hours without food at the Civil Lines Police Station in Karachi while the government prepared its case against us. Some high-ranking people in the government were involved. My father had orchestrated the whole thing. He wanted the government to deal with me decisively once and for all.

The government's case was finally presented, and the news wasn't good.

"You are found guilty of distributing anti-Islamic literature, indulging in anti-Islamic activities, anti-Pakistan actions, and disturbing the public peace and order. You are to be held in detention for ninety days, further extendable by an additional ninety days."

I knew what that meant. I was going to jail.

Soon, they moved us to the Karachi Central Jail, where we were kept in the ward reserved for political prisoners.

Once in the prison, we were issued worn and filthy blankets encrusted with the dried vomit of previous prisoners. These were our beds, which we made on the rough, uneven brick floor. The five of us shared a single, filthy, little cell.

Breakfast was a mug of tea with a "chapatti," a flat, round flour tortilla that is a dietary staple in Pakistan. These chapattis, unfortunately, were made of flour that was full of sand. Lunch and dinner consisted of cold boiled liver or lentils or vegetables accompanied by the sand-impregnated chapattis.

The toilet—if one could call it that—consisted of two small concrete blocks to squat on, with a shoebox-size metal container resting on the floor between bocks. The toilet sat in the corner of the cell. There was no privacy.

> *I was in prison just as the apostles had been. . . . I felt it a privilege and honor to walk in their footsteps, to be counted worthy to suffer for Jesus.*

It was oppressively hot. Mosquitoes and other insects feasted on our blood. Nevertheless, we rejoiced, counting it an honor to be imprisoned for the gospel.

I was overwhelmed that unworthy though I was, God had favored me, counting me worthy of the privilege to suffer for my Master and Savior. I was in prison just as the apostles had been. The price for their preaching was imprisonment. Why should it be any different for me two thousand years later? I felt it a privilege and honor to walk in their footsteps, to be counted worthy to suffer for Jesus.*

After a few days, the four brothers who were with me were discharged. They were foreigners, and their embassies had obtained

---

* During those days, I thought all Christians went to prison for the gospel, that it was part of the normal Christian experience. After my release, whenever I met other Christians, i would introduce myself as "just released from prison for the gospel" and then ask them when they had been in jail.

their release. The Pakistani government deported them, and I was left alone in prison. Several times I was chained to other prisoners and taken to the local courts for trial. We waited for hours, but nothing ever happened. The court system never called my case. They held me without benefit of trial.

The conditions in the huge prison were appalling, with drugs and homosexuality rampant among the prisoners. The ward I was in was somewhat safer. The prisoners were mostly political prisoners, with the exception of two men being tried for murder. The political prisoners came from various political parties that opposed the government.

For safety reasons, foreigners who were arrested were also incarcerated in the political prisoners' ward. I remember two Germans who were brought in for attempting to smuggle narcotics. As they introduced themselves to the other prisoners, one of the politicians from a militant party jumped up and began to shake one German's hand, trying to make a positive impression by shouting, "You German. Allah is great. I like German. German great people. You had great leader like Adolf Hitler. What a great man. If Pakistan have leader like Hitler, we would be a great nation, too." The poor red-faced Germans were just too embarrassed to respond.

I discovered a legal clause through which I could get out on bail. The government responded by charging me with some far-fetched, fabricated violations. On paper, at least, it is not illegal to preach the gospel in Pakistan. Pakistan claims to be a country with full religious freedom. This made it difficult for them to prosecute me for becoming a Christian or for preaching Christ. To get around this, they had to create a charge in order to keep me locked up.

This time they informed me that under the Defense of Pakistan Rules, I was to be "detained until further orders." This was the same as saying, "We're going to lock you up and throw away the key." The government in Pakistan has laws that allow them to lock people up for indefinite periods on undefined or vaguely defined charges of being "a terrorist," "anti-Pakistan," or "anti-Islamic," giving the detainee no access to any legal recourse or a chance to defend himself or herself.

I was now, according to the government, an "illegal alien," a foreigner who had entered the country for "subversive activities." I had no access to a lawyer, and it was impossible for me to prove that I, contrary to the charges, was indeed a Pakistani citizen. This was because my passport and ID documents had been confiscated earlier, making it impossible for me to prove my identity. I met some innocent prisoners who had been held for years under this particular clause.

I wrote to the General Headquarters Army, to the air force, to my father's friend General Zia-ul-Haq, later president of the country but then chief of staff (army), telling them that I was being held illegally and requesting that they send documents proving my true identity. I got no reply. By this time I had been in prison for over two months. I have no idea as to the actual total time I spent in prison, since I was not allowed a watch or a calendar. All I know is that one month passed after another. I spent almost the whole of 1976 in prison.

Alone in prison, with no one to encourage me and with the days, weeks, and months creeping by, I found myself sitting down and taking stock of my life. What value did my life have? I sat in prison, having lost everything. Society looked upon me as a disgrace. In my life, I had seen so many ups and downs, storms and upheavals. Once I was without hope, but then I found hope in Christ—but had I found Him? Really found Him?

Was Jesus real? Was He with me now in my time of trial, or was this just another foolish thing I had done with my life? If it was another one of my follies, then things were tragic indeed. I had lost my inheritance, my place in society, and the last bit of claim I had on my family. I surrendered everything. But if Jesus was truly the Savior, the Son of God, then I had won eternal life.

> *There is no material thing valuable enough to live for, and I decided to turn my back to all that this world has to offer. Nobody could prevent me from preaching the gospel of Jesus. I had everything to gain and nothing to lose.*

I needed to know. I desperately needed to know that Jesus was who the Bible said He was and that He had not forgotten me. If Jesus is the Son of God, then the price I was paying was worth it all. That would make me like the man who found a pearl of great price and sold all that he had in order to obtain it.

Then the sweet presence of my Master filled my mind and heart. I knew He was there. I sensed His holy presence beside me and in me. The glory of God filled that bleak prison cell. Suddenly the verse in Matthew 25:36 came to me. It says, "I was in prison, and ye came unto me."

"Jesus is alive," I whispered to myself. "Jesus is with me. He lives in my heart. I am truly a child of God. One day I will be with Jesus in heaven for all eternity."

That day God put His seal upon my life, and I have never looked back. I knew beyond doubt that Jesus is the Son of God and that He is faithful and true. I knew that I had died and risen with Christ into a new life that no man could take away. From that moment onward, my life was no longer my own but His. I would live for Him and serve Him with all my heart. Jesus was all that was worth living and dying for. There is no material thing valuable enough to live for, and I decided to turn my back to all that this world has to offer. Nobody could prevent me from preaching the gospel of Jesus. I had everything to gain and nothing to lose.

That day God set a mark on my heart. I decided to live for

Jesus without reservation or hesitancy. From that day on, it was all or nothing.

Although I was a "baby" Christian, having known Jesus only a few months, and was alone without any Christian fellowship, the presence of the Lord sustained me. In my loneliness, He was there. I bore witness for Jesus among my fellow prisoners. One person with whom I shared my faith was a young man of Anglo-Indian parentage named Ginger. He had killed a man and was waiting for execution. After sharing my faith with him, he prayed to receive Christ. He could leave this world knowing what awaited him on the other side.

Just a few months old in the Lord, I felt humbled, yet thrilled, that He had counted me worthy to experience what the apostles went through in the Book of Acts. What an honor to be called to walk in the footsteps of the Master, to bear my cross and to follow Him.

Perhaps I would be one of the martyrs and lay down my life for Jesus. I would then say farewell to this world and go to be with the Lord. At times the martyr's call seemed to beckon me, but that conflicted with what Jesus had said to me earlier about sending me all over the earth to tell people about Him.

I was torn between heaven and earth. I wanted the martyr's crown so much, yet I knew that I had to live to do the will of God. But then, although to do the will of God on earth was wonderful, it was even more wonderful to be with Jesus. I had had an unhappy life before Jesus, and this world had nothing that attracted me to it. I wanted to be with Jesus more than anything else, yet the call of the gospel also burned strong within me: to live on, so that others may also live.

I struggled with these conflicting desires. I finally chose to live, to yield myself to God to do His will. At times I still am torn between heaven and earth, but as I see the multitudes of people come to Jesus when I preach, I understand that I did the right thing. The yearning to be with Jesus is a painful longing that tears at my soul. I would rather be in heaven today than on earth, but I'll stick around until God's plan with my life is fulfilled. Then one day, after I have preached my last message and finished my course, I shall drop this robe of flesh, put on garments of glory, and rise from this earth to be with my Jesus. What a glorious hope Christ gives us. But until then I will live for Jesus with all that is within me.

After almost a year of humiliation, I was suddenly being treated like a VIP.

I remember being thrilled to my bones and rejoicing as I read in the Bible, "And they departed from the presence of the council, rejoicing that they were counted worthy to suffer shame for his name" (Acts 5:41).

Upon the advice of a fellow prisoner, who was an attorney imprisoned for political reasons, I wrote my father informing him that I would file a *habeas corpus* in the high court challenging the government for wrongful imprisonment if he did not get me out immediately. I would ask for General Zia-ul-Haq and other senior military officers to come and identify me. The charges against me would be proven false, and my accusers would be held accountable.

My father, upon receiving my letter, came immediately with a release order. The deputy warden himself came to give me the news of my release. After almost a year of humiliation, I was suddenly being treated like a VIP. They brought loads of cakes and other goodies to me, which I distributed among my fellow prisoners.

The day after my release, a senior police officer came to the place where I was staying and informed me of the limitations and restrictions that were imposed upon me because I had been a political prisoner under the Defense of Pakistan Rules. First, he told me I had lost several basic rights enjoyed by every citizen—even though I was never convicted of a crime. I no longer had the right to hold a passport or to leave the country. Second, I was put in my father's care and placed under his full authority. I was required to live with him in Lahore. Third, I could not leave the city limits of Lahore without permission. And the final restriction, I was not allowed to own a Bible or to meet with any Christians.

If I broke any of these conditions, I would be sent to prison again. People living in Western nations may not understand this, but that is how the legal system worked in Pakistan. The law was overruled and manipulated at the whims of the powerful, while those without influence had no choice but to submit.

In spite of these circumstances, I knew that God would somehow bring me through. Still, I knew the days ahead would be difficult.

Chapter 7

GOING UNDERGROUND

〜

I WENT TO LAHORE with my father and had to live in his house. I was not allowed to get a job as I wanted; I was under his complete control.

My father had received a farm from the government because he had attained the rank of general in the army and had also been decorated for bravery. He often sent me out to watch over the farm and keep an eye on what went on there. My father would pay the bus fare and nothing more, so I never had extra money.

The farm was in a wild and lawless area of Punjab Province. The people in the area were known as "Junglees," meaning "the wild people." They had illegally occupied huge tracts of government land for decades, and no one dared evict them. They were cold-blooded murderers and armed to the teeth. Because of this, the government provided no irrigation or electricity to the area. These people were renegades, and even the police feared them. Murders were common.

There was no law and order. These people had a tribal code of ethics, and with that came an odd view of what was considered good and admirable. Young men, for example, had to prove their manhood by stealing somebody's cattle or by committing some other noteworthy crime. Only then would they be considered worthy to sport a mustache or be eligible for marriage. In their twisted culture, a prison term was the highest accolade because it meant that one had done something illegal and was thus a real man among men.

> *I found it hard to imagine Jesus shooting someone even in self-defense. What could I do?*

How my father took possession of his farm is a story worth telling. My father had been told by the army that he could choose any piece of land he wanted from all government lands in the country. Upon making queries as to where the best land lay, he had been told that this particular lawless area was one of the most fertile and therefore most sought after tracts in the entire country. He was also told that many others had been allocated land there before him, but nobody could ever take possession because of the violent nature of the Junglees.

My father, ever gifted with boundless imagination, devised a cunning plan. He moved one of his anti-aircraft artillery regiments to the area for maneuvers. The regiment rolled in with their 37 mm light antiaircraft guns, 12.7 mm quad LAA guns, and other blood-chilling weapons. Gun-pits were dug in the farmers' fields, and the guns were then deployed as the locals watched with wide-eyed fear. A command post was set up, and hundreds of soldiers spread over the area. Jeeps with machine guns mounted on them drove around the area. Pakistan Air Force jets then flew in making low passes over the area, while the guns traversed, practicing "dry laying" on them. It was quite a show.

The hitherto fierce locals, though well armed with rifles, pistols, and shotguns, were frightened out of their wits by this display of superior firepower. The sight of the big guns was too much for them. To enhance the effect, my father also sent a number of handpicked noncommissioned officers (NCOs) among the people spreading the word that it was dangerous business messing with this general. The locals, out-muscled and terrified, decided that capitulation would be their best course of survival. They welcomed us to the region and did not resist the possession of our land.

What my father wants, my father gets.

At the farm, I slept in a hut and was always armed with a rifle or shotgun. I never went to sleep or ventured outdoors without a loaded weapon by my side. The locals would test me often to see how far they could push me. They would steal small amounts of our grain and make mischief to test the limits and to intimidate.

Before I had met Christ, I used to go to the newly acquired farm. I used to swagger around the farm with my weapon and act tough. It was the only way I could assert myself and gain their respect. I had arranged for people to be arrested and beaten. On one occasion, I attacked someone's house and come close to shooting them for sending their dog out to harass our sheep. Our shepherd boy had come running to me complaining about this, and I had taken my gun and gone straight to the house of the people who had done this. I stood outside shouting to them to come out so that I could shoot every one of them. The only thing that stopped me from killing them that day was their pleas for mercy. My blood boiled with rage, and I remember being shocked at myself. It is amazing how violent a person can get living among people who do not value human life. The locals considered me a dangerous man, and they feared me.

Now that I was back as a Christian (although they did not know that I now followed Jesus), it posed a real dilemma for me. I needed to have the peoples' respect, yet I did not want to threaten, intimidate, or to shoot anyone—not even in self-defense. I found it hard to imagine Jesus shooting someone even in self-defense. What could I do?

One day they found out that I had recently been released from prison. Not knowing that I had been to prison for the gospel's sake, they promptly assumed that I must have done something bad to get such a sentence. They did not dare ask me why I had been in prison. In their minds, going to prison was the ultimate sign and achievement of manhood. I was now a man among men, and one to be feared. One of them said to me, "You were in prison. Only the bravest among the brave end up in prison."

After word spread, I had no trouble with Junglees. I could walk around unarmed and without having to intimidate anyone.

Months passed, and my father did desperate things to force me back into the Muslim belief. He forced me to go to the local army mosque, where I was made to go through the gymnastics of Muslim prayer. What they did not realize was that I was praying to Jesus. One of my father's friends offered me his attractive, young daughter in marriage if I would become a Muslim again. I declined the offer. My father then offered me his wealth or anything else I wanted. I could have a beautiful wife and my own business if I wanted, but all I wanted was to leave and follow Jesus. They could not understand why I would choose Jesus over wealth and a beautiful bride.

Another thing they could never understand was why I had left Islam. "What fault do you find with Islam? Why do you have to leave our religion and follow a foreign religion? Tell us, what is wrong with Islam?"

We must let Jesus grip us, and when He does, He gives us the faith, the will, and the power we need each day. We can then walk through fires of life without being burned.

My answer always was, "I have nothing against you or Islam. I do not even think on these lines, but you must understand that Jesus has seized my soul. He has taken hold of my life. He is calling me. He has given me peace, joy, and love, and He has set me free from my sin and misery. I would gladly do anything to please you, but I cannot deny someone who is so wonderfully real and close to me like Jesus. I would be a fool if I denied Him. Please understand."

They never did.

One of my father's closest friends, a general, once said to me, "Ah. All young men get drunk, smoke pot, sow their wild oats, and live on the wild side. It's normal, but then they grow up, get a job, marry, and stabilize. You don't need this Jesus. Come on, just think of your future. Get real."

Nothing was more real than Jesus. It was He who made me real. Everything I did and was prior to that moment of salvation was artificial. That was reality. I had made my choice. For me it was Jesus alone, and nothing else.

To understand what I am saying, you has to experience a real, red-hot, blood-washed salvation, truly knowing Jesus as a living reality, knowing that you have passed from death to life, that your sins are washed away, and that your name is written in the Lamb's Book of Life.

We must let Jesus grip us, and when He does, He gives us the faith, will, and power we need each day. We can then walk through fires of life without being burned. Jesus grants us the victory. This is what distinguishes true salvation in Jesus from dead religion.

I could not carry my Bible openly. If seen, I would be immediately arrested. I had to find a solution to this problem. I took a ninety-minute audiocassette and taped Scripture on one side and secular music on the other. I would listen to Scripture, and if someone came along, I would turn the tape over and turn on the music. I also had a small pocket Bible hidden under my mattress that I read every day.

OUT *of* ISLAM

I was an underground Christian in my own father's home. As such, I still managed to make contact with other Christians. I must say here that with a few exceptions, most Pakistani Christians in Lahore generally treated me badly, and that hurt me. For some reason they suspected my motives and found it hard to believe that I was truly a believer. Some believed that I was pretending to be a Christian because I was in love with a Christian girl and that I would go back to Islam as soon as I had married her. Despite the public accusation, no one could identify the mystery girl. The fact that I had been to prison for my faith did not put a dent in their prejudice against me.

When I could, I would sneak out and attend services at a local church. It should have been a source of joy for me, but instead their rejection wounded me. What hurt the most was their refusal to allow me to partake of Communion. Whenever there was the Lord's Supper, I was instructed by the pastor and other church leaders to sit in the last row away from those who were allowed to receive Communion.

As I see it, the reason for this shabby treatment was that in spite of generations of missionary work, Pakistani church leaders and churches are spiritually dead and have no faith that Muslims can come to Jesus. Most of the bishops and pastors in the country are petty, corrupt, and money-hungry; they act more like politicians than men of God. They are mostly nominal Christians and do not value the salvation of sinners. They do not take the gospel to the Muslims. Worse, they loathe Muslims because of the way they have treated Christians for generations. I could not find a single Pakistani pastor in Lahore who was willing to baptize me. They either believed that a Muslim could never come to Jesus, or they were just too afraid to baptize a Muslim convert because of the persecution that would inevitably follow.

*The devil may have come to destroy,
but Jesus, the mighty Deliverer, came to
destroy the works of the devil.*

I was vindicated years later when, after living many years overseas, I traveled to Pakistan and ended up preaching at the annual Lahore Convention, a big meeting attended by thousands. I recognized several of the people there who had treated me inappropriately in earlier days. One of them was now a big church leader and by amazing coincidence was my interpreter when I preached. (My colloquial Urdu was never good enough for preaching because it was not my mother language at home.) They saw that the Lord's hand was upon me. I went up to them afterwards and introduced myself. I could not help but notice their embarrassment and shame at meeting me, and several of them tried to save face by saying that they had no recollection of me. I was satisfied that they at least now knew that I was a genuine Christian and not an imposter. That was enough for me.

George and Anne Tewksbury, Presbyterian missionaries in Lahore, were two of the few who showed me love and kindness during those difficult days. I would visit them as often as I could get away. I badly needed their Christian fellowship and encouragement. George and Anne, though busy missionaries, always made time for me.

Their ministry was difficult, working with young American and European backpackers bound by drugs. They took many of these addicts, some of who were insane, into their home. It was heartbreaking to see these young people in the clutches of the devil, their minds and bodies destroyed every day by the drugs they took. Most of them came from wealthy homes where they received everything a person could want—except love.

One young man who came to George and Anne was Francois, the son of a French official in Greece. Drugs, especially LSD, had eroded Francois' sanity. One night, his brain filled with mind-altering drug, he stripped off his clothes and ran through the streets of Lahore stark naked. Some of the city's citizens caught him and beat him. A Christian on the scene managed to rescue him and brought him to George and Anne.

The devil may have come to destroy, but Jesus, the mighty Deliverer, came to destroy the works of the devil. In the Book of Amos the Word of God says that if a lion devours a lamb, even to the point where only one ear and two legs are hanging out of the lion's mouth, the Lord can still bring deliverance (Amos 3:12).

I saw Jesus set people free from the jaws of death. I recall one particular girl named Karin from Austria. Just twenty-seven years old, she had been on heroin for ten years. Her husband had recently died of an overdose. She had the appearance of an old woman: unkempt, stringy hair; tired, expressionless eyes; and several gaps in her smile where teeth had once been. George and Anne ministered to her with such tenderness, praying with her, until she was set free of her bondage to the drug. I remember her face, radiant with the light of the Son of God, as beautiful as an angel, tears streaming down her cheeks as she sang and played at George and Anne's piano.

Karin went back to Austria and married. A few years later she and her husband returned to Pakistan as missionaries—proof again that Jesus is a wonderful Savior. Karin's testimony of God's grace encouraged me and strengthened my faith in the Lord Jesus.

George and Anne taught me much and prayed with me often. They were people with great spiritual power yet infinitely meek, tender, and always compassionate. At times I would tell George what I was going through. He would hold my hand and weep, tears streaming down his cheeks. The love and the strength of God that they imparted into my life kept me going.

My father finally found my New Testament hidden under my mattress. To make things worse, that particular day was the festival of Eid al-Fitr, one of the holiest days of the Muslim year. He was furious.

The police came that evening, arrested me, and took me to the police station. They set out a few chairs in the front yard, and my father and the police officers sat while I was made to stand like a common criminal on trial. A crowd soon gathered to see what was happening. My father and the police officers berated me for having become a Christian and for reading the Bible. They called me names, humiliated me, and insulted me. The people who had gathered also joined in the shouting, expressing shock that the son of such a great man as my father could do something so terrible. They made it clear: I had disgraced the family honor.

> *My becoming a Christian had cost him his honor, and he desperately wanted to win it back.... The only way he could obtain that now was by killing me himself or having me executed.*

After a time, my father took me aside. His anger had grown, and he let loose his pent-up fury, dicing me with his words. It was as painful as anything I had experienced. He used a filthy invective referring to the Lord Jesus—words I can't write here, words I wish I could clean from my mind. I snapped. For the first time in my life I did something unthinkable in that culture: I stood up to my father. "Don't you talk that way about Jesus. You don't realize who He is. He is the Son of God."

This, for him, was the last straw. He had done all he could to reform me and had failed. There was only one thing he could do. I could see the hatred and disgust in his eyes. He said, "We have taken the soft approach with you, but I see now that nothing can change you. You should be beheaded."

I could not believe what I heard. I looked into his face and saw a murderous glint that I had never seen before. This was my own father. His words "You should be beheaded" echoed in my head like close thunder, and it struck me that he meant what he had said. He wished I were dead. My becoming a Christian had cost him his honor, and he desperately wanted to win it back. He wanted Allah's favor and Muslim society's respect. The only way he could obtain that now was by killing me himself or having me executed. Only by taking my life could he fulfill the requirement of Islam, please Allah, and wash the stain of dishonor that I had brought upon him.

For a moment I stood in stunned silence. A second or two crept by, then I looked him straight in the eyes and said, "All right, go ahead and kill me. I know Jesus is taking me to heaven, but you do not know where you are going. You may kill my body, but you can never, ever kill my soul."

That night I decided the only way out for me was to leave the country. Political unrest had flared in Pakistan. Massive demonstrations filled the streets, and the police were shooting and killing people by the hundreds. As was the practice, anyone who had ever been arrested under the Defense of Pakistan Rules was being rearrested. This meant that I, who had been a "political prisoner," could be arrested and imprisoned at any time, for no reason, and for an indefinite period. The police had warned me earlier that this would happen to me if I continued to possess or read a Bible.

Those were turbulent times in Pakistan. Islamic fundamentalists were on the rise, and their political parties were gaining strength at an alarming rate. In a few weeks, General Zia-ul-Haq, my father's friend, would stage a coup d'état and overthrow the government. Prime Minister Zulfiqar Ali Bhutto would be arrested, tried for ordering the murder of political opponents, and hanged. The masses were in the streets demanding Islam, Islam, and more Islam. Religious leaders spoke openly and demanded total adherence to Islamic law. One Muslim leader even said on national television that any Muslim converting to Christianity should be executed. So, on the one hand I was threatened by imprisonment once again, and on the other, my own father had just threatened to have me executed.

I had been thinking about leaving the country for some time, but I was not sure if that was God's will for me. It would perhaps be a far better thing to die for my testimony of Jesus; after all, God had given me everything that I had ever wanted. I had peace, love, and joy that only Christ could give. I had a place in heaven. Jesus had said in John 14 that He was preparing a place for me. There is no greater honor for the believer than a martyr's crown, and it would be mine. I was willing to stay and die.

Still, there was one factor that kept rising in my mind. Just three days after my conversion I had heard God say, "This is what you shall do the rest of your life. I shall take you all around the world, and you shall tell people about Jesus." Once again, I was facing the prospect of death for the sake of my faith in Jesus. Once again, I struggled with the same choices as I had when I was in prison: should I go to be with Jesus, or should I live to bear the cross and serve Him on earth?

I believed Jesus had plans for me. He wanted me to preach this gospel to others who were as bound as I once had been. I was torn between heaven and earth but could not ignore the message I received. I understood what God's will was for me. I was going to live and not die.

The thought still comes to me that how much more wonderful it would be for me to walk with Jesus on those streets of gold. Surely it would be better than this world, where we stumble, make mistakes, and are under pressure from all sides. But then I think of the countless souls I have been able to lead to Jesus since then and the multitudes of chains that still need to be broken. Still so many people are captives of Satan, people whom we must set free.

I missed the martyr's crown, but I had a mission to fulfill. All Christians have the same mission. If we live, we have to live counting the eternal destinies of sinners as being of greater worth than what we desire for ourselves. We have to preach this glorious gospel to the sinners for whom Jesus died, because Jesus alone is mankind's only hope. I dedicated myself again to the work of evangelism.

By then all my money was gone. I was penniless and knew no one who could help me get out of the country. I was, however, convinced that it was God's will for me to leave Pakistan as soon as possible, so I knew that He would somehow make a way.

I shared with George and Anne Tewksbury that the time had come for me to leave. They prayed with me, and together we committed my journey into the hands of God.

Chapter 10

ESCAPE

ARLY ONE SPRING morning in 1977, as dawn spread over Lahore, I made my escape with the help of some sympathetic Muslim friends. I had known Jesus for only sixteen months, but those days had been filled with severe persecution. I had been in a mental institution, arrested several times, imprisoned for almost a year, and threatened with execution. Now, finally, I was on my way. I had the equivalent of seventy-five cents in my pocket. God told me to trust Him to meet my needs and not to ask anyone for money.

Carrying my backpack, I first went to see Pastor Aslam Khan to ask for his help. Pastor Khan was a true warrior for Jesus, a man looked upon as an apostle and spiritual general. He had spent his life preaching the gospel and winning souls. He was seventy-six and was still immersed in ministry. Every morning he rode his old, creaking bicycle to far-off places to preach and to pray for people, returning home late in the evenings. I stayed with Pastor Khan for some time, and it was quite an experience.

Pastor Khan pulled me out of bed at 4:30 every morning and would order me to wash my face with cold water. This would snap me awake. He would then take me to the tiny chapel that he had built on the grounds his house sat on. He would take the platform, and I would sit in one of the two pews. There were just the two of us there, but as far as Pastor Aslam Khan was concerned, there might as well have been a congregation of a thousand present. He would start with prayer and then lead the congregation (that was me) in a rousing chorus, punctuated with shouts and resounding hallelujahs. It did not bother him that I didn't know the words to the songs he sang. After this he would ask me to take the pulpit and read a word of Scripture, while he took the pew. Once I had read the passage, we would then trade places again, and he would preach a fiery sermon. He would then command me to get down on my knees, and we would end the service with a long time of prayer, often with his hands on my head. This was our daily routine.

He surprised me one day by ordering me to preach, which I nervously did. I have no recollection of what I said, except that I was shaking with fear and that Pastor Khan shouted "amen" and "hallelujah" through the entire sermon, short as it was.

In those early days of my Christian walk, Pastor Aslam Khan was an example of fiery faith. He went to be with his beloved Jesus some years ago. I can picture him today walking on the golden streets of glory, his loud hallelujahs shaking heaven itself.

Pastor Aslam Khan blessed me and bought me a train ticket to Karachi, where I stayed with some Christian friends. I learned that a countrywide search was going on for me, but I was well hidden by this family. Years later I discovered that my father had gone to the inspector general of police, the highest-ranking police official in the Punjab province, and had told him what he wanted done to me.

"Catch him," he said, "and when you do, you have my permission to kill him—hang him if you want." A shoot-on-sight order was issued.

The Christian family with which I was hiding managed to get

me a passport and gave me five hundred dollars, which in Pakistan was a small fortune. I stayed with them for over a month, and they treated me like their own son. During this time one longtime desire I had was fulfilled—I was baptized. James Turner, a Southern Baptist missionary from Kansas, was a fearless man who loved Jesus. He baptized me in the Arabian Sea. It is a dangerous thing to baptize an ex-Muslim in a Muslim country, and the person doing so puts his own life at risk, just like the Muslim convert.

Pastor Turner was murdered four months later in Murree in the Himalayan foothills. The killers were never caught, and the authorities never gave an official reason why he had been killed. Believers in Karachi who knew him, however, knew that he was killed because he had baptized me. I owe an incalculable debt to James Turner, who laid down his life for me. The only way I can even begin to repay that debt is by laying down my life for the gospel of Jesus. Nothing less is worthy of the price that James Turner paid for my sake.

Checking for countries where I could travel to on my Pakistani passport, I found out that it was impossible for a Pakistani citizen to go anywhere without a visa, with the exception of Turkey. Also, it was practically impossible to get a visa for anywhere, except Afghanistan. Not being left with many choices, I made up my mind that I would go to Afghanistan, then to Turkey, and finally westward to a "Christian" country. I still had the notion commonly entertained by people in my part of the world that "all white people are Christians." With this belief, I assumed that I would certainly be welcome in Christian nations like England or the United States. All I wanted was to live in a place where I could read my Bible, worship, and serve God in a peaceable way without facing arrest for doing so.

I applied for an Afghan visa, and the embassy of Afghanistan stamped a ten-day visa in my passport. I paid one hundred twenty dollars for a one-way air ticket from Kabul in Afghanistan to Istanbul in Turkey via Moscow on Aeroflot, the Soviet airline.

This was the most inexpensive ticket that I could find. The reason I did not buy an air ticket directly out of Pakistan was that there were stringent checks of every departing passenger at all international airports. Leaving the country overland was always easier. After I had made all my plans, I then found out that it was illegal for a Pakistani citizen to take U.S. dollars or other foreign currency to Afghanistan. I decided that I would hide my money in my socks when I would cross the frontier into Afghanistan.

I owe an incalculable debt to James Turner, who laid down his life for me. The only way I can even begin to repay that debt is by laying down my life for the gospel of Jesus.

I then caught a train to Quetta, a large city over six hundred miles from Karachi and about seventy miles from the Afghan border. My plan was to cross the border into Afghanistan, go first to Kandahar, and then to Kabul. From Kabul I would fly to Turkey and there see what the Lord had in store for me.

Meanwhile the manhunt for me was still on.

After a thirty-six-hour train ride through the Baluchistan desert, I arrived in Quetta, praying that I would not be caught by the police and that God would make it easy for me to get out of the country. Then, by what I call a "blessed coincidence," I ran into the company commander from my old battalion. He was now serving in a battalion in Quetta. We were good friends, and we had shared a bunker when I was with my battalion in Kashmir. He had heard rumors of what had happened to me and knew that I was being hunted by the army and the police. He then insisted that I stay at his home where I would be safe. So there I was, safely in an army officer's house in a military cantonment while a manhunt for me was going on.

My ex-commander put me in touch with another officer, an artillery major, who was commanding troops in Chaman, the town where the Pakistan-Afghan border crossing was. I was told that he would help me because of his special relationship with our old battalion. He had been the artillery battery commander supporting our battalion with artillery fire during the battle of Leepa Valley in Kashmir, and I remembered him as a regular at our officers' mess. By divine providence, he was at the border that I needed to cross in order to get to Afghanistan.

I arrived in Chaman by bus and went straight to the army officers' mess. I met the major, who happened to be in civvies when I arrived. He invited me to join him for lunch, but I was eager to get out of Pakistan as soon as possible, so I declined his kind offer of hospitality, thanking him anyway. We walked straight to the Pakistan Police and Immigration checkpoint to get me across the border. There were two officers on duty. Both sat in battered metal chairs. The first officer, who apparently couldn't be bothered to rise from his seat, examined my passport and shook his head.

"I can't let you pass," he said.

"Why not?" I asked. My heart skipped several beats. "All of my papers are in order."

"You need a no objection letter."

"No one mentioned such a letter," I protested. "I've never even heard of such a thing."

"You need a letter from the police station in your home town stating they have no objection to you leaving the country. You don't have one, so I can't let you pass."

"But—"

He cut me off. "It is the law. There is no way around it."

I fought back my frustration. I hadn't expected this. To make matters worse, I caught sight of the policeman's partner thumbing through a thick file. I got a glimpse of photos and written descriptions. I suppressed my fear, afraid that any display of anxiety would make them suspicious. It was hard to do. I knew my picture and description were in that file.

I was moments from discovery.

My friend, the major, still in civilian clothes, was losing patience. He had been quiet while I tried to argue my way across the border, but he finally identified himself and said, "This man is my friend, an officer, and he is going through right now. I shall sign a paper on his behalf. Send it to my office tomorrow, and I'll put my official stamp on it."

Realizing who he was, they shot out of their chairs, came to attention, and saluted. They stamped my passport and let me through without delay. I praised God for helping me.

The next obstacle was the Pakistan customs post. I knew that they, as a matter of routine, asked everybody to declare any foreign currency that one might be carrying on his person. I had my U.S. dollars hidden away in my socks. I knew that if I told the truth, I would be arrested immediately for contravening foreign currency laws, but I was uncomfortable with lying. I was in a dilemma, and in silent prayer I committed the matter to my heavenly Father.

> *Just when it looked like there was no chance of me getting a ride with them, they turned to me and said, "OK, hop in. We shall take you to Kandahar."*

We walked from there to the customs post, the last place I had to pass through to leave Pakistan. When I finally stood before the customs officer, he looked at me and asked, "Are you Mr. Alam?"

Another surprise. "Yes, I am."

He nodded then marked my backpack with a small X with a piece of chalk. "I have just received a telephone call and have been instructed to let you through without any questions. Please proceed."

I was stupefied. Even the major looked stunned. Who could

have called this customs officer? Nobody else but the two of us knew that I was there, and the major assured me that he had not made the call.

Then I understood. It must be my heavenly Father. For a moment I imagined that somewhere near His throne He has a telephone for special situations like this one.

The Pakistan customs post was in the middle of the desert, and between there and the Afghan immigration point-of-entry lay a few miles of no man's land. I learned something new. There was no public transportation, and no one was allowed to walk across. One had to be in private transportation in order to pass.

I stood there wondering how I would ever get to Afghanistan. As these thoughts coursed through my mind, the major and I noticed two gentlemen who had just driven up to the customs post in a new Mercedes-Benz with diplomatic license plates and flying an Iranian flag. They stepped into the inspections area where I stood to show their passports. This was the consul-general of Iran and his personal assistant. With no other visible alternative, I mustered my courage, walked up to them, and asked for a ride across the border.

At first they stared at me, as if they could see into my mind. What I was doing was outlandish. They then began to look me over from head to toes, inspecting me as if I were a medical specimen in a laboratory. I knew what they saw: a longhaired, unshaven hippie wearing grubby jeans and carrying a backpack and guitar. I certainly did not look like the kind of fellow any diplomat in his right mind would give a ride to in his new Mercedes. They stepped away and conferred among themselves, all the time keeping an eye on me. As they discussed in their native Persian (which I understand in bits and pieces), I picked up a few words like *hashish* and *hippie*. They were concerned that I might be smuggling drugs.

Just when it looked like there was no chance of me getting a ride with them, they turned to me and said, "OK, hop in. We shall take you to Kandahar."

Kandahar was the first big city on the road in Afghanistan. From there I had planned to take a bus to Kabul to catch the flight to Istanbul, transiting through Moscow.

I got in the Mercedes, and we drove off. We soon arrived at the Afghan immigration checkpoint. The officers on duty, wearing gray uniforms with "Dieu est mon droit" inscribed on their belt buckles, glanced at the Iranians' diplomatic passports and saluted. They then looked at my Pakistani passport, at me, and at the Mercedes. I knew exactly what they were thinking—I didn't fit.

The officer, closely examining my Afghan visa, slowly shook his head and said that my visa, unfortunately, was not in order because the dates written in English did not match the ones written in Persian. Under no circumstances could they let me into Afghanistan. I would have to go back to Pakistan and obtain a new visa.

While I struggled to think of something to say, the Iranian diplomats spoke up for me. "This man is our friend and is with us. You have to let him in, and we shall take the responsibility to see to it that everything is sorted out right."

The officers stood in uncertain silence, then saluted. They returned my passport and waved us into Afghanistan.

"Thank You, Jesus," I whispered, as we drove into Afghanistan at the foot of the majestic Spin Boldak Mountains. I took deep a breath of freedom. God was with me, and I was at long last out of Pakistan. He had used Pakistan army officers, a mysterious telephone call, and Iranian diplomats to get me out. That was plenty of proof that He was with me.

Chapter 11

HELP FROM THE KGB

༄

E ARRIVED IN Kandahar a few hours later, where my new-found friends the Iranian diplomats insisted on dining me royally in two nice restaurants. They then put me on the overnight luxury bus to Kabul and even paid for my ticket.

I arrived in Kabul early the next morning and checked into a cheap little hotel on the famous Chicken Street. This is where all the hippies and backpackers stopped and stayed when passing through the city. Kabul was a beautiful and exotic city, surrounded by high mountains. The city center was alive with people from around the world. People were friendly, and it was like no other place I had ever been. I began to see why everybody I had met who had ever been to Kabul liked the place so much. The centuries-old city center oozed history and culture. The newer parts just off the city center had wide tree-lined boulevards. The weather was wonderful. All kinds of fresh fruit and good food were available everywhere. It was also inexpensive, and at the moment, that was very important to me.

Despite the idyllic setting, there was tension in the air. The monarchy of King Zahir Shah of Afghanistan had been over-thrown not long before in a coup d'état led by his cousin General

Sardar Daoud. Troops patrolled the streets now and then, but the people could generally move about freely as they pleased. Sadly, there would soon be another coup, this time by Communist hardliners supported by the Soviets. Sardar Daoud would be overthrown, Afghanistan would be thrust into a long series of bloody wars lasting decades, and the beautiful old city of Kabul would be ravaged.

My first step was to locate the local Children of God group. I finally found them, but after only a short time with them, I sensed there was something terribly wrong. It was hard to say what it was exactly or to express what I felt in words, but something just did not seem right. It could be, I reasoned, that I felt this way because I had not had any contact with them for so long.

At first, I let my suspicions slide. I asked one of the brothers for the Mo Letters I had missed. Mo Letters were weekly leaflets, letters, and booklets containing the teachings of the leader of the Children of God, Moses David. These were published with instructions indicating whether that particular letter was for general reading, for leadership only, or for higher leadership only. The Mo Letters I had seen in my time with the Children of God in Pakistan had been the basic kind. Now, in Kabul, I was given a stack of Mo Letters to read. I was horrified. I was shaken. Most of the letters were nothing but filthy pornography, some encouraging prostitution, fornication, and adultery, while others were downright blasphemous.

I felt hurt, lonely, and most of all confused. My brain swirled in emotions. It was through these people I had come to know Jesus. How could this happen? What could cause these wonderful brothers and sisters to sink so low into the pit from which they once had been set free?

Regardless of my past positive experiences with them, I knew I could no longer identify myself with them.

Reeling from this shock and desperately in need of Christian fellowship, I began to look for more "normal" Christians. God led me to some foreign believers who worked at a Christian eye hospital in Kabul. I visited them, and they received me kindly into their home. I shared with them that I was going to Turkey, and they gave me the names of a couple who were working there as underground missionaries. They did not have an address to give me but hoped that I would somehow be able to find them once I got to Istanbul.

I went to the local office of Aeroflot, the Soviet airline with which I held a ticket. I wanted to reconfirm my seat on the flight. A lady at the Aeroflot office checked my ticket and informed me that I would have a four- to five-day layover in Moscow in order to catch my flight to Istanbul. She also told me that I needed to obtain a Soviet visa, as visas were mandatory for layovers longer than twenty-four hours. I was referred to the Soviet embassy.

The embassy was a large complex surrounded by high walls and a perimeter of sandbags and coils of barbed wire; it sported machine-gun emplacements at regular intervals. With my heart beating faster than usual, I entered the embassy and went to the consular section, where I applied for a visa. The consular officer took one look at my passport and turned my application down on the grounds that my Pakistan passport was not endorsed as valid for travel to the USSR. For this reason I would not be granted a visa.

I had run into a brick wall and couldn't see any way around it. I went back to my hotel room wondering what to do next. I did the best thing I could—I fell on my knees before God. I prayed long and hard for help. The last thing I wanted to do was tangle with the Russians. I had just finished reading a book called *Vanya* by Myrna Grant, telling how brutally the Communists persecuted Christians in Russia. It was horrifying reading.

I went back to the Aeroflot office. It was common knowledge that Aeroflot offices operated as fronts for the KGB and were staffed by their agents. As such, one had to be careful in any dealings with the company. Entering the Aeroflot office, I went to the same lady to whom I had spoken earlier and told her that I had been refused a Soviet visa. This time I took notice of her name tag: "VICTORIA."

> *I had a five-day visa issued in about ten minutes—something that normally took two weeks to get. Once again I was reminded: with God, nothing is impossible.*

She told me that without a Soviet visa, I would not be allowed to board the flight for Moscow. Furthermore, my ticket was non-refundable and could not be changed to any other airline. I would lose the money I had paid for my ticket. If I could not get a visa, that was the end of it, and she could do nothing.

Then I did something that surprised even me. Without thinking I said, "Madame, I want you to know that I am a Christian and have escaped from Pakistan where I was persecuted for my faith in Jesus Christ. If you do not let me go to Russia, I shall be sent back to Pakistan where I face prison and death, and it will be your fault."

The words tumbled out, and I could hardly believe my ears.

She stared at me for a few seconds. "Wait a moment." She got up from her desk and walked over to a smartly dressed man who sat behind a large desk in a glass-walled office. He seemed to be the supervisor. I could see them talking, gesturing, and pointing at me.

The man stepped out from behind his desk in the glass-walled office and walked up to me. He and the lady smiled. I didn't know if I should trust the smile.

"Everything is going to be OK," he said. "Don't worry." He picked up the phone, called the Soviet embassy, and spoke to someone in Russian. Turning to me, he said, "Just go to the embassy to the visa section. Somebody is waiting for you there, and you shall get the visa."

It took a moment for the news to sink in. That was it. I could stroll over to the embassy again, and my visa would be waiting for me? It seemed too good to be true, but over the last year I had learned not to doubt God's ability to intervene.

What a miracle! I praised the Lord all the way to the embassy. He used Pakistan army officers, He used Iranian diplomats, and now He was using the KGB to get me through.

Back at the Soviet embassy, a gray-suited gentleman was waiting for me; he received me as if I were a visiting dignitary. Like in a dream, I filled out the visa application forms. Overwhelmed by this miracle, I did not fully grasp what was going on, but I had a five-day visa issued in about ten minutes—something that normally took two weeks to get.

Once again I was reminded: with God, nothing is impossible.

I boarded the Aeroflot aircraft at Kabul Airport. Victoria, the Russian girl at the Aeroflot office, came to see me off. She was warm and sweet and wished me all the best as I boarded the jet. I had laid bare my soul to her. It was an act of desperation wrapped in faith. Instead of condemnation, I found courtesy and much needed help. Victoria is the feminine of "victory" in Latin, and God used her and her supervisor to grant one more victorious step to my journey.

I arrived in Moscow the next day. Aeroflot took me by bus to their transit hotel in the city where they gave me a room and coupons for complimentary meals at the hotel restaurant.

Hungry, I decided to go to the restaurant for lunch. As I walked into the restaurant, I noticed that every table was taken. But right by the door where I stood was a table set for six, with three people seated and three empty seats. I was famished and didn't want to wait for a table to become available. One of the three men seated at the table was studying me. He had a pleasant appearance, dark hair, and a goatee. I asked if I could take one of the empty seats.

"Sure," he said. "Make yourself at home."

As soon as I sat down, the man started a conversation. He showed an unusual interest in me and asked probing questions. "What is your name? Where are you traveling from? Where are you going?"

His questions made me nervous.

I was not eager to answer his questions. After my hair-raising reading of *Vanya*, I felt I should be careful around Russians. This man looked like the KGB-type to me, and I had no desire for a one-way trip to a prison camp in Siberia.

He pressed me with more questions, and I was no more comfortable about lying here than I was at the border crossing. At first, I answered in generalities, but he pressed harder. I feared if I answered too vaguely I would look suspicious. Finally I let the truth out: "I am a refugee fleeing persecution for my faith in Jesus."

There it was: the truth laid out on the table as visible as the plates and utensils.

I waited for his reaction.

There was a pause as the goateed man studied me some more. Then a broad smile split his face. "Brother, praise the Lord!" He grabbed my hand and shook it vigorously. "I am also a Christian."

I let loose a sigh of relief.

"Where are you from?" I asked.

"Sweden."

With his dark hair and beard, he didn't look Swedish to me. Before I could say anything else a memory surfaced. An American Baptist missionary in Pakistan had told me, "If you ever run into any Swedish Christians from the Orebro Mission, ask them to help you. They are Baptists and are good people."

"Do you know of the Orebro Mission?" I asked, hopeful.

His jaw dropped. The spaghetti he was eating dropped out of his mouth and back onto his plate.

"Why do you ask about Orebro Mission?"

I told him about the American missionary's comment about the Orebro Mission.

He pulled out his wallet and handed me his business card. It read: "Thord-Ove Thordsson, General Secretary, Orebro Mission."

An electric thrill ran through me. Jesus had not ceased to amaze me with the way He was leading and straightening my path for me. He brought me all the way to Moscow, the world headquarters of Communism, to meet a minister of Jesus Christ from Sweden, the very man that I needed to meet.

Thord-Ove then said, "You do not know this, but I saw you at the airport in Kabul yesterday. We were on the same flight to Moscow. I sensed that there was something special about you; I felt an urgency in my heart to speak to you, but the timing was never right. There were too many people around. I lost sight of you at the airport in Moscow and thought that I would never see you again. When you walked into the restaurant and asked to sit next to us, it became clear to me that God was in all this, and I just had to find out who you were. Now I know. I am flying on to Stockholm and want us to keep in touch, and I shall help you as much as I can." He gave me his contact information.

Thord-Ove and I had wonderful fellowship in Moscow. We worshiped, prayed, and partook of the Lord's Supper together in my hotel room. He gave me some U.S. dollars as a gift and paid for my hotel room for the rest of my stay, as Aeroflot gave me only one night's free accommodation. We then parted ways. He flew on to Stockholm, and I to Istanbul, Turkey.

Chapter 12

ISTANBUL, TURKEY

ARRIVING IN ISTANBUL, I headed straight for the famous Pudding Shop at Sultan Ahmet, a well-known gathering place for hippies, backpackers, and adventurers of all kinds headed eastward to India or westward to Europe. I had been told earlier that for first-timers in Istanbul, the Pudding Shop was the best place to find one's bearings. On the recommendation of a fellow backpacker I met there, I found a room in a cheap hotel in the vicinity.

I found out quickly that the area was infested with shady characters, criminals, smooth-tongued hustlers, and unsavory types of all kinds. Many looked as if they walked straight out of a Humphrey Bogart movie. They were openly dealing in narcotics and black-marketing stolen passports and travelers checks. One Pakistani at the hotel offered me a British passport with a German residence permit stamped on it, an air ticket to Germany, plus four hundred pounds sterling, if I would only deliver a package for him to a friend in Germany. It was obviously a drug smuggling operation, so I declined.

Father Luigi spent two entire days with me, feeding me at his expense, praying and encouraging me, and trying to find the missionaries whom I was searching for.

I wanted to find the underground missionary couple that the Christians in Afghanistan had told me about, but I had no address. It would be difficult because Istanbul is a large city of several million people, and few spoke English. German was more common, but my German, at best, was bad. It would be a daunting task, akin to looking for the proverbial needle in the haystack. I also wanted to get away from Sultan Ahmet as fast as possible.

I started looking for a church. I walked for hours around town and was chased away from Greek Orthodox churches by priests who shouted at me. I finally found a Roman Catholic church. Tired and worn out, I sat down on the steps outside. It was peaceful and quiet. I could hear beautiful sacred music being played on the organ inside. Overwhelmed and lonely, I began to weep.

A young man from the church saw me, approached, and started a conversation. I asked him if I could see a priest. He took me to Father Luigi.

Father Luigi, a kind American priest, took me to a little office and first fed me a hearty meal before asking me what I wanted. I told him my story and gave him the names of the underground missionary couple that I wanted to find.

Father Luigi spent two entire days with me, feeding me at his expense, praying and encouraging me, and trying to find the missionaries whom I was searching for. We traveled all over Istanbul, visiting different people and places and asking about the missionaries. We finally found them. They were Americans and taught English to the locals. They received me warmly into their home and treated me as a member of the family. I stayed with them for three weeks. They were kind, loving, and hospitable.

While in Istanbul, I encountered the Children of God again. I felt terrible just being around them and battled with my conflicting emotions about them. On the one hand, if it weren't for them, I would probably never have heard about Jesus. I would still be a depressed and embittered young man—I might also be dead by my own hand. But on the other hand, they had lost their first love and now seemed full of unclean spirits, which to me was unacceptable and intolerable. Yet, my bonds with them were so strong; I could not break away from them. I owed them so much.

I then found out that they had a new doctrine that advocated the women in their group to prostitute themselves "to win converts." I also saw a Mo Letter in which Moses David proudly took credit for the recent great air disaster in Tenerife. I knew of the disaster. Two fully loaded 747s had collided on the runway at the airport, and hundreds had lost their lives. Moses David had fled from there sometime earlier, and he claimed that the air crash was "divine retribution" upon the Canary Islands.

I was sickened by all this and shared my problem with the missionary couple I was staying with. They advised me to break with the Children of God completely, decisively, and with all my heart.

I struggled with it, but because I loved Jesus so much and wanted to distance myself from evil, I made a decision to renounce all my ties with them. It was painful. I wrote a letter to my old Children of God leaders, who then happened to be in Dubai in the United Arab Emirates. I urged them to repent from their sin and turn to the Lord. Furthermore, I informed them that I no longer wished to be associated with them. It hurt to break bonds with those who had led me to the Lord, but my love for Jesus led me to put Him first in all things. After I had taken this step of breaking free, I felt a new sense of purity and freedom.

∽

The American couple with whom I was staying arranged for Operation Mobilization (a missions organization for youth) to invite me to their annual summer campaign and conference in Leuven, Belgium. I was given a ten-day Belgian visa, and with the remainder of my money, plus a gift from my American hosts, bought a ticket to Brussels. The Lord was certainly making a way for me, but I suddenly realized I was facing a major problem.

It was 1977, and European countries required that visitors arriving from third-world countries show they possessed at least two hundred dollars upon arrival to ensure that they were bona fide visitors and not penniless illegal immigrants. The trouble was that I had only about seven dollars left after paying for my ticket.

When I left Pakistan, the Lord had impressed upon me that I was not to ask anyone for money. I took great care not to advertise my financial needs but to trust God alone. I prayed and committed the situation to my heavenly Father.

With great assurance in my heart, I went to Istanbul's Yesilkoy Airport and checked my luggage in on the Sabena Belgian Airlines flight to Brussels. Clutching my passport and boarding pass, I stood in the check-in area. My financial need hovered in the background. I needed two hundred dollars. God had to do something and do it fast.

"Hi, brother." A loud voice from behind jarred me from my thoughts.

I turned around to see who it was. It was an American Southern Baptist whom I had met a few times in Istanbul. He was a friend of the couple I had stayed with. Once he invited me to his place for a meal. He knew nothing of my financial need. In fact, during my visit with him I said very little. He talked incessantly, preaching to me that "the King James Bible is the only true Bible." I had breathed a sigh of relief upon leaving his home that evening. Now here he was again.

"I heard you were leaving today," he said, "so I felt in my heart that I had to come to see you off."

He had come all the way to the airport to see me. I was surprised. Yesilkoy Airport is a long way from Istanbul. It was nice that a Christian brother would think of me and make the sacrificial effort to see me off.

We chatted for a few minutes, and then it was time to say goodbye. We shook hands, and I felt some paper rustle in his grip.

"I just felt that I had to give you this," he said as he pressed the paper into my palm. He then turned and walked away. After he was out of sight, I opened my hand and looked. It was two one-hundred-dollar bills. I began to praise God and danced all the way to the waiting aircraft.

A Baptist had just given me a "Pentecostal handshake."

Jesus again met my needs.

Chapter 13

OPERATION MOBILIZATION

AFTER I ARRIVED at the airport in Brussels, I went straight to Operation Mobilization's headquarters in the village of Zaventem not far from the airport. I was warmly received there by an Englishman who took me to Mickey Walker, the team leader. Mickey Walker was a bearded Californian—a 1960s' "Jesus revolution" type—friendly, warm, and welcoming. He would prove to be a great encouragement to me in the days to come. I doubt he would remember me today. I was just one of the many people who passed through his life and whose hearts he touched. As we sat and talked in his office, I felt that God wanted me to give away all my money, right there and then, down to the last cent I possessed. I promptly emptied my money pouch and stood once more with nothing.

I got my visa extended and spent two months with an Operation Mobilization summer team in Ostend, on the Belgian coast. Many teams were sent all over Europe, and we had been the last ones to leave the base. The teams were sent out with stocks of food for their needs, but when our turn came almost nothing was left. We had to take whatever little was available. So off we went with a few boxes of cornflakes, a few jars of jam, and a box of cucumbers.

Once in Ostend, we had to trust God for our food. At times we would get loads of cakes from the brother of our Belgian team leader, a baker, and chicken from a local butcher. We would roast the chicken and follow with the cakes. Other times we would pick mussels from the mussel beds by the beach. At other times we had to improvise and make do with whatever was available.

With us was a Chinese brother from Singapore. He often cooked a delicious fish-head soup. I found it quite tasty, but then again I was brought up on Middle Eastern delicacies like lamb's brains, eyeballs, and tongues. For the Europeans and the Americans on the team, it was a very different story; they did not quite exhibit the same level of enthusiasm for Brother Soon's Singaporean fish-head soup as I did.

"I want to show you how much Jesus loves you. If you receive the Lord Jesus, I will stand before your friends and take the beating for you. Would that convince you that Jesus loved you enough to die for you?"

We were on the streets every day ministering to people. We handed out gospel literature, shared testimonies, and sang. It was the summer holiday season, and thousands of people from all over Europe were there. We ministered daily on the beautiful beaches of the picturesque coast of Flanders. Every home in the province of West Flanders received a copy of the Gospel of Mark from us.

We lived in an old house two blocks away from the beach in Ostend. We slept on the floor in sleeping bags, with ten of us in a room. Our team consisted of twenty-eight people living in three rooms. We ministered together, ate together, prayed together, and had Bible studies every day. Although all twenty-eight of us shared the same bathroom and personal space was limited, there was never strife. There was joy and excitement in the team because we were doing what we all loved to do more than anything else—telling people about Jesus.

There were drug-dealers and others who took offense to my testimony and what I shared in the street meetings. Some of them called me names, threatened me, and did their best to intimidate me. I preached strongly that Jesus could deliver drug addicts from their bondage.

I remember one young man named Jean. He had used heroin for many years and rode with a motorcycle gang. He looked fierce with long, dark hair down to his waist, ever-present wraparound mirrored sunglasses, and a black leather jacket covered with steel studs. He came to our street meetings and would stand glowering at us. I managed to make contact with him and shared the gospel with him every day. He was as hard and cold as steel and said little. One day, as I talked with him, he took his sunglasses off. I was amazed as I looked into his eyes. Never before in my life had I ever seen such hard and ice-cold eyes, devoid of any sparkle of life or joy. The days went by, and I kept after him, witnessing and sharing with him about Jesus.

Then one day, as I was talking to Jean, God let me see him as he was: bound by fear and torment. I said to him, "Jean, you want to receive Jesus, but there is one thing holding you back, and that is fear. You are afraid that if you give your life to Jesus, your motorcycle-gang friends will beat you up with knuckle-dusters and chains, isn't that true?"

He looked down at the ground and nodded silently. At that moment the love and compassion of Jesus filled my heart, and I put my arm around his shoulder.

"Jean," I said, "Jesus suffered so much in order to save you, no suffering that we endure could ever match the intensity of His pain. I want to show you how much Jesus loves you. If you receive the Lord Jesus, I will stand before your friends and take the beating for you. Would that convince you that Jesus loved you enough to die for you?"

His eyes welled over with tears, and right there on the beach promenade, Jean knelt on the ground and asked the Lord Jesus to come into his heart. Fortunately, I never had to appear before his friends.

The next day he came to our house and asked one of the team to give him a haircut. He said, "I don't want to look like Absalom anymore."

He accompanied us to church that Sunday. There was a light in his eyes—he was a new man. The Bible says, "If any man be in Christ, he is a new creature: old things are passed away; behold, all things are become new" (2 Cor. 5:17).

After the summer evangelistic campaign in Belgium was over, I spent one month with friends in the old fishing village of Urk in the Netherlands, then it was back to Belgium again.

My time in Operation Mobilization was fruitful. I was privileged to get to know George Verwer, the founder and leader of the movement. George was and still remains a man of strong faith and great vision, imparting to thousands of youth a vision for the lost. He maintained a powerful emphasis on surrendering one's life to God for the sake of the gospel.

Talking about the biblical principles of material prosperity without putting emphasis on living lives of self-denial, sacrifice, and putting the cause of the gospel foremost in our lives amounts to nothing but spiritualized greed, selfishness, and the lust for material things.

As an American, he constantly hit the "cult of softness" produced by the materialistic culture of America. He was right. I know America to be one of the richest nations on earth. Most Americans are wonderful people, but many have become of little use for the gospel because they have made the quest for material things the primary goal of their lives. When the pursuit of the material becomes more important than the pursuit of the spiritual, a great deal is lost.

On a per capita basis, churches in America send fewer laborers to the mission field than many other nations. Churches in countries such as Norway and Holland send a much higher percentage of their people and money to the mission field. This is because the version of Christianity practiced in America is the shallowest and the hollowest in the world, and it does not cost anything to call oneself a Christian. Because of this, few in America are prepared to lay down their lives for the preaching of the gospel in foreign lands if it would mean giving up some of the material comforts of this world.

I must emphasize that I believe strongly in financial prosperity as the Bible teaches it. However, talking about the biblical principles of material prosperity without putting emphasis on living lives of self-denial, sacrifice, and putting the cause of the gospel foremost in our lives amounts to nothing but spiritualized greed, selfishness, and the lust for material things. People should realize that God wants more than just their money. He wants their hearts.

Not only that, but at times God may want us to forsake some of the good things of this world so that others may have that which is far more excellent, namely, the knowledge of Jesus Christ our Lord.

George Verwer lived a simple lifestyle, and his one driving passion was the spreading of the gospel to the world. He left an indelible impression on my life and lit a fire in my heart that still burns. During my days with Operation Mobilization, I dedicated my life anew to the work of the gospel worldwide.

Chapter 14

SWEDEN

AT THE END of three months in Operation Mobilization and as the summer drew to a close, I began to contemplate my future. I was still a refugee, a man without a country and without a place to go. In the midst of my contemplations, I received a letter from Thord-Ove Thordsson, the Swedish man I had met in Moscow. He had been working hard to help me get a visa to Sweden and was pleased to inform me that the Orebro Mission, together with the Capernwray Fellowship of Torchbearers, had granted me a scholarship to attend the Torchbearers Bible School in Holsby-brunn, Sweden. It was an English-language school whose student body was comprised mainly of overseas students.

It is said that Swedes are like a bottle of ketchup: you shake and shake and nothing comes out. But if you're patient, it all pours out suddenly.

I went to the Swedish embassy and was granted a visa, but I still did not have any money to travel to Sweden and did not want to advertise my financial need. The Lord had taken care of all my needs during this time, but I did not have any extra cash at hand. Once again I put my trust in the Lord and knew that He would take care of me.

Things began to happen.

I began to get envelopes stuffed with money from anonymous donors. I believe it was God blessing me for giving away the two hundred dollars I had when I first came to Belgium. I soon had a sizable sum of money, plus an offer of an all-expenses-paid ride to Sweden in an air-conditioned Mercedes-Benz.

On September 23, 1977, I arrived in Sweden in style, praising the Lord for His goodness.

I fell in love with Sweden. I thought then and still think today that it is one of the loveliest countries on earth. I found Swedish believers to be shy, yet warm, friendly, and generous once I got to know them. Swedes are hard to get to know, but once a Swede is your friend, you have a friend for life. He or she will stand with you through thick and thin. Swedes do not know of superficial friendships. It is said that Swedes are like a bottle of ketchup: you shake and shake and nothing comes out. But if you're patient, it all pours out suddenly. It takes time to get to know them, but once you know them, they open their hearts to you.

One thing that impressed me was the Swedish Christian's strong sense of separation from the world and commitment to God. In many other countries, it is socially popular to be a church-goer. Most church attendees do not have that strong sense of being separated from the world. For them, it is fashionable to say, "I am a Christian." In Sweden, however, it is the other way around. Churchgoing is not fashionable. It is looked upon as something for people who are out-of-step with modern times. They are viewed as relics from the Middle Ages or as being feeble-minded. Those who call themselves Christians in Sweden are committed to the faith and live lives separated from the world. Though generally not emotional people, I saw in the Swedes a depth of commitment, faithfulness, and Christian love that I have always found precious and beautiful.

The Torchbearers Bible School where I was enrolled as a student was situated right in the middle of the scenic and thickly wooded countryside of Smaland in southern Sweden. Most of the students were Mennonites from Canada and Baptists from California and Washington in the United States, with a sprinkling of other nationalities plus a few Swedes. Some of the Swedes had told me and the other foreigners that the woods were thick with polar bears and that we should be careful, because polar bears often roamed on the streets of the nearby town of Vetlanda (where we went on weekends). It took me several months before I found out that they were pulling my leg. Only then did I ever dare venture into the woods alone.

I had never yet received any teaching on giving, tithing, or receiving financial blessings from God, but I had learned the value of living a life of charity. I had a lot of money that I had received while I was in Belgium and felt uncomfortable keeping it all for myself. It was, after all, God's money. The Lord prompted me to anonymously bless other students with the cash. I secretly put money into their mailboxes. Amazing things began to happen. I discovered that the more money I gave away, the more I received, as a result of which I never lacked anything and always had enough for "extras" for myself and to treat my friends. I learned that we can never out-give God. He always blesses abundantly.

My time at the Torchbearers Bible School was good, although my heart was not set on the theoretical parts of the teaching that I felt had no practical value. Because of the influence Operation Mobilization had on my life, I was focused on soul-winning. Looking back, I can see that at times I acted immaturely and even foolishly, but my instructors at Bible school were generous and forgiving. I was not one of their best students, but they continued to encourage and correct me.

I participated in as many evangelistic outreaches as I could, witnessing on the streets of the nearby town of Vetlanda, on trains, in schools, in prisons, and in church-run coffeehouses. I even managed to get a team to minister aboard a U.S. Navy destroyer docked at the Royal Swedish Naval Base in Karlskrona.

At the end of my year at the Bible school with my Swedish student's visa about to expire, I had to think again of my future. I did not want to continue indefinitely as a refugee. A letter had reached me from Pakistan, saying the authorities there knew of my whereabouts, that my Swedish visa was soon to expire, and they were expecting me to return immediately. I also learned an army officer had visited the Christian family that had helped me escape and had questioned them.

I took this to the Lord in prayer and then decided to seek political asylum in Sweden. My goal, initially, had been to go to an English-speaking country. I did not speak a word of Swedish, and the Swedish language had, it seemed to me, certain humanly unpronounceable sounds. There were, for example, about half a dozen different variations of the pronunciation of the *sh* sound. Sometimes *ja*, which is Swedish for *yes*, would be spoken while inhaling through the mouth, making the speaker sound rather like an asthmatic. This was unnerving. I had no desire to learn Swedish, but I felt that God had brought me to Sweden. I loved the country and the wonderful Swedish Christians. I had developed deep friendships—friends who are still close to me today. They helped me through their kindness, love, and generosity. I am grateful to the Lord for them, for my teachers at Bible school, and for the many other wonderful people who prayed for me, encouraged me, and left a lasting memory of blessings in my life.

I went to the local Swedish police station and applied for political asylum on the grounds of religious persecution in my home country. I also moved to Uppsala, a town about forty-five minutes north of Sweden's capital city, Stockholm. An attorney in Uppsala was assigned to my case: Mr. Peter Nobel, a descendent of Alfred Nobel, after whom the Nobel Prize is named. A well-known attorney, he was to present my case to the Department of Immigration. I was told that he was the top lawyer in Sweden concerning immigration cases.

I had several long sessions with Mr. Nobel, in which he interviewed me in detail in order to present a strong case on my behalf. Mr. Nobel had the bearing and polished manners of an English gentleman and spoke like an aristocrat. He was a kind, intelligent, eloquent, and sympathetic man and highly esteemed in his profession. The United Nations considered him an expert on international refugee politics.

We went through the details of my case several times. In the end, when he had prepared my case, he pointed out several important legal aspects to me. He also told me that my chances for getting political asylum in Sweden were practically nil. He gave several reasons. First, according to the 1954 Geneva Convention for refugees, a person seeking asylum had to do so in the first signatory (to the convention) country that he came to after leaving his home country. In my case, that country had been Turkey. Furthermore, I had traveled in Belgium, the Netherlands, Germany, Denmark, Norway, and Finland before I applied for asylum in Sweden.

The next reason was more disturbing: the one seeking asylum had to apply within forty-eight hours of his arrival in the country. I had been in Sweden for eight months before contacting the police.

Third, there was no known persecution of Christians in Pakistan. The Swedish embassy in Pakistan had not reported any Pakistani persecutions. That was understandable, since diplomats on foreign soil rarely venture to where people lived. Their view of Pakistan was limited and inaccurate. It was possible that they knew of no persecution because they seldom left the embassy grounds.

The information they sent to their government was incomplete and lacking personal observation. Regardless of the reasons, as far as the government was concerned, I did not come from a country with a recognized "refugee problem."

> *She shook her head. "Your only chance is this: go to a discotheque, meet a girl, start living together, and you'll easily get residence and work permits. Then you can stay in Sweden."*

To a certain extent, that was true, because there had never been a mass persecution of Christians. They were discriminated against in many ways and were treated like second-class human beings by the Muslim majority, but they had never been persecuted in the true sense of the word. At the same time, Muslims who turned to Christ would normally be killed by their own relatives, but the number of these cases was not large enough to attract international attention or interest. These cases were never reported by the news media. In many ways, it was a real problem but also an invisible one.

Mr. Nobel made these factors clear to me. Two other factors influencing the negative attitude of Swedish authorities toward Pakistani refugees were the media reports of thousands of Pakistanis seeking political asylum in Germany on fraudulent grounds. They were being deported back to Pakistan by the planeload. Also, a couple of years earlier, a Pakistan Air Force aircraft had come to Sweden in an official capacity to fetch spares for Swedish SAAB training aircraft used by the Pakistan Air Force, and Swedish authorities had found smuggled drugs aboard the aircraft. Pakistani citizens did not enjoy a high level of credibility in Western Europe.

I visited an organization of lawyers in Stockholm in order to get some additional advice. A lady lawyer whom I met with asked me bluntly, "Do you have a Swedish girlfriend?"

"No," I answered.

She gazed at me as if I was abnormal. "So long in Sweden and no girlfriend?" She shook her head. "Your only chance is this: go to a discotheque, meet a girl, start living together, and you'll easily get residence and work permits. Then you can stay in Sweden."

It was my turn to shake my head. "I'm a Christian. I can't—I won't do what you ask."

"Look, when it comes to matters of life and death, you have to put religion aside. It's time to be realistic."

"God has brought me so far, and He can take care of me. But if I am deported back to Pakistan and am killed, I know where I am going when I die. I'm prepared to accept that fate, but I will not do what you suggest just to get to stay here."

She frowned. "I'm only trying to help. You do it your way. If it does not help, you can always come back here…"

She didn't need to finish the sentence. I left her office, went out on the street, and wept. My tears blurred the sights of beautiful Stockholm. Passersby stared at me. I lifted my face to heaven and shouted, "Jesus, help me. I trust You. I want to be faithful to You unto death."

The devil will always present us with opportunities to compromise and to take what seems to be the easy way out, but Jesus, the One the Bible calls faithful and true, is the way. God's way is always the right way.

> *The Father has given to Jesus all power in heaven and on earth. This makes impossibilities possibilities and puts the miraculous power of God within our reach.*

As he mailed off my case to the Department of Immigration, Mr. Nobel told me that I should be prepared for a very long wait. I anticipated this, having known a number of refugees in Uppsala who had been waiting as long as two years, some even more, to get a decision on their cases.

In addition, Mr. Nobel advised me to be "realistic" and not be too optimistic. But reality, to the child of God, is that Jesus, the King of kings, is upon the throne. The Father has given to Jesus all power in heaven and on earth. This makes impossibilities possibilities and puts the miraculous power of God within our reach. When our lives are committed to God, He works wonders on our behalf.

My parting words to Mr. Nobel were that I was trusting Jesus. I then settled down to wait for the Department of Immigration to make their decision, having no idea how long it would take.

Four days later, I received a letter from the Department of Immigration informing me that I had been granted residence and work permits in Sweden. It was four days since Mr. Nobel sent in my case, and it had taken them only two days to decide in my favor.

Everyone said it was a miracle. Some, however, were skeptical and assumed that somebody in the government must have made a mistake. Such a thing was unheard of—nobody had ever been granted political asylum so quickly. They called the Department of Immigration to ask about this and were told that it was not a mistake. They had looked at my application the hour the documents had reached them and had made an immediate decision to grant me political asylum.

The Bible says, "The king's heart is in the hand of the LORD, as the rivers of water: he turneth it whithersoever he will" (Prov. 21:1). This means that God has the power to give us favor with authorities and to turn their hearts to our benefit.

I thanked and praised the Lord for His goodness and provision for me. My long journey had brought me all the way to this wonderful country. I would now have a place to call home. Since the day I met Jesus three years earlier, I had experienced persecution, abuse, rejection, imprisonment, and much more. Each time, Jesus granted victory. Through Him we are surely more than conquerors.

Chapter 15

SETTLING DOWN

∽

I BEGAN TO SETTLE down in my new homeland. The government put me into a language school to learn Swedish. I dreaded it at first. But immersed in a Swedish-only situation, I began to pick it up quite well, even learning some of the difficult sounds that I was certain were beyond my abilities.

I began attending an evangelical Lutheran church that had a strong outreach to immigrants and foreign students from Muslim countries. The effort was led by two ministers, and I joined them to help in whatever way I could, mainly in going out to evangelize Muslims. Today I realize that I was more of a nuisance than a help. These two men were meek and loving people. I spent a lot of time with them and their families.

I also became active in the young adult group. It was good to be involved with people my age and to have friends to hang around with. It was in this circle that I met a pretty girl studying nursing at the local university. Her name was Britta, and she came from a small community in the far north region of Sweden close to the Arctic Circle. The people there speak Swedish with a soft, lilting accent.

If I had my way, we would have married right away. The Bible says, "It is better to marry than to burn," and around me one could smell smoke.

Britta had been a strong Christian since childhood. She was pure and faithful to Jesus and had always been eagerly involved in the things of God. I noticed her tender spirit and the air of sweetness she exuded. At first we were just friends. But then on a trip to England and the Netherlands, I found myself being attracted to her more and more. I fought to suppress my feelings; I had, after all, decided to live single forever like the apostle Paul. I wanted to live alone, going around the world for the gospel, just my backpack and me. I watched my concrete resolve dissolve into mist. It wasn't long before I had to acknowledge the truth: I was absolutely crazy about Britta. Just being near her made my heart pound and my knees turn to jelly. There was no doubt: I was head over heels in love.

God began to work on me, and I began to see Britta as His special gift to me. It took a while, but I finally worked up enough courage to express my feelings to her. Despite a dry mouth and sweaty palms, I revealed my love for her. It was a wonderful surprise to hear that she felt the same way about me. Now we were officially—as they say in Sweden—"together." We began to spend a lot more time with each other.

If I had my way, we would have married right away. The Bible says, "It is better to marry than to burn" (1 Cor. 7:9), and around me one could smell smoke. However, after what to me looked like a decent wait of four months, I decided to ask her to marry me. I had prepared a big speech and planned to propose on my right knee, but my throat would turn dry every time I wanted to pop the question. Finally, one day, in the most casual way, I said, "Hey, let's go and get us some rings, eh?"

So much for the big proposal I planned.

She accepted, and we were officially engaged on May 18, 1979, and were married six months later on November 18.

As our relationship grew, I felt the need to share an important truth with her. "I love you very much," I said, "and I would rather spend the rest of my life with you than with anyone else. But you have to know this: I have the call of God on my life. There will come a day when I will be gone often preaching the gospel. I cannot offer you a cozy, normal life, and though I love you very much, Jesus will always come first in my life. If you accept this, we can get married. If not, it's better we call it off, no matter how much it hurts."

Britta accepted without reservation. Today she is my wife, my soul mate, and, apart from Jesus, my best friend. I love her more than words can tell, and I would not be what I am without her love and support. The Lord has blessed us with three wonderful children—Immanuel, Victoria, and Gabriel. To Jesus I give all the glory for putting her by my side and for blessing me with such a wonderful family.

After I finished my language studies in mid-1979, I believed I was ready to get back into full-time ministry. I had the calling since I first received Jesus over three years earlier, and I had been ministering full time since then, except for this short time in Sweden when I was only part time in the Lord's work. Now I wanted to return to full-time ministry. However, God directed me to a secular job instead. In Uppsala, jobs were scarce, but the Lord led me to ask my Swedish language teacher for help. She referred me to one of her friends who promised me a job.

I imagined I would get a fancy job, but instead I was offered a position as a janitor. It was humbling. I came from a well-to-do family, and as I was growing up, we had our own janitor who cleaned our house. As a child I could remember having seven servants at my beck and call. I had never cleaned floors, and now I was doing servant work. My pride was further injured by

Britta's work—she was a registered nurse and brought home a larger paycheck. All my friends had wonderful jobs—and I was a janitor. I felt humiliated and ashamed.

Then the Lord spoke to me. He told me that before He could use me as He desired, I had to first humble myself and learn to get my hands dirty. I did the work for the next thirteen months. Over that time the Lord brought me to a place where I was proud to be a janitor. I cleaned those filthy and stinking bathrooms, toilets, and floors with enthusiasm. It was a great life lesson for me. I learned the dignity of labor and that God looks not at a person's social status but at the heart. He is not a respecter of persons or of worldly fame or position. If we are proud of what we are in the world, He has to bring us down and break us before He can use us for His glory.

I took pride in my work. The people who worked in the offices I cleaned complimented me on my work. I felt like Michelangelo being praised for painting the Sistine Chapel.

Chapter 16

AND THEN THE FIRE FELL

As I CONTINUED along my journey of faith, something began to bother me. I had met many Christians and attended a variety of churches, but a key element seemed to be missing—the lack of supernatural power in the church. The New Testament account is filled with accounts of God's supernatural power in the lives of His people. Wonders and miracles are shown in abundance in the pages of the Bible, but I had yet to see that kind of power in any church that I knew.

Where was the power? The subject often came up in sermons and Bible studies, but the ministers I heard always put forth highly intellectual and bombastic theological discourses explaining why God's supernatural power was not available today. Healings and miracles were relegated to today's medical treatments, and prophecy was explained as nothing more than "good teaching." To me such thinking amounted to a cover-up of unbelief. There was a lot of preaching about why God did not do the same things today as He did in New Testament times; no one, it seemed to me, was teaching how to experience God's power for today. Even soul-winning, which I felt to be the heartbeat of God, was of minor importance.

It seemed the church lived only for itself in its self-serving theology, to entertain its members and to maintain the status quo. I also had to face the truth that my life lacked evidence of spiritual power. While I became disenchanted with powerless churches, I also became unhappy with my own Christian development. That sword cut both ways. I witnessed for Jesus as often as I could, but I saw few results. That frustration led to difficult questions and a deep longing to drink from the well of God's power.

> *I concluded there could be no "baptism with the Holy Spirit." Except for the noise and the shaking, I seemed to have the Holy Ghost as much as any Pentecostal or Charismatic I knew. They were just as powerless as I was.*

Some told me that the answer was "baptism with the Holy Spirit," an act that seemed to set people called Pentecostals and Charismatics apart from other Christians. I took a closer look at these groups and noticed the following: they spoke in tongues, prophesied at times, jerked, shook, and generally made a lot of noise. But when it came to real power, they were as just as impotent as the rest of us.

"Where was the real power?" I asked myself. "Was this baptism with the Holy Ghost just noise and nothing else?"

The Charismatics and Pentecostals I knew seemed to believe they were superior to other Christians and were going to heaven as first-class believers while the rest of the body of Christ was flying coach. The Bible calls such thinking "pride." Despite their claims of power, I never saw it.

It was not (and is not) my intent to mock others. I was brought up to be a pragmatist and have remained one my whole life. And I was being pragmatic. If God meant for His power—the same power of New Testament days—to be used by His servants today, then searching it out was more than curiosity; it was duty. The apostle Paul wrote, "For our gospel came not unto you in word only, but also in power..." (1 Thess. 1:5). I heard the words, but I could not see the power, and it began to eat at me.

As an ignorant and young Christian, I concluded there could be no "baptism with the Holy Spirit." Except for the noise and the shaking, I seemed to have the Holy Ghost as much as any Pentecostal or Charismatic I knew. They were just as powerless as I was. I concluded that salvation and baptism of the Holy Spirit were the same event.

As time passed, I became obsessed with the topic. My lack of understanding festered in me. If anyone brought up the topic in my presence, I became argumentative and angry. Another emotion began to plague me: depression. Rooted in my still active sense of insecurity and compounded by my growing frustration over unanswered spiritual questions, depression would roll over me like waves from the ocean. Every week I became more desperate, and that desperation fueled my growing depression. I desperately wanted to see God's power in the world and in my life.

A few months later, I heard of Harry Greenwood, an English minister who used to hold meetings in Sweden. He was reputed to be a man familiar with the power of God. Greenwood was holding services in a large Methodist church in Stockholm, so Britta and I decided to go and see for ourselves what was happening. The church was almost full when we arrived, but we managed to get seats near the front.

The first thing I noticed was the joy that permeated not only the worship but also Harry Greenwood. During the service, he held a large tambourine and played it like I have never seen anybody play the tambourine—all with a wide, infectious smile on his face.

He preached a lively message and then spent about thirty minutes pointing to different parts of the crowd.

"There, in the back, near the corner, is a woman with a problem in her kidneys. The Lord has healed you, sister."

His eyes shifted to the front of the congregation.

"Here is a man deaf in his left ear. You are healed by the power of Christ."

On it went—blindness, broken bones, and every imaginable illness. He called them out, and God healed them.

I watched in fascination. As he would point and call out the people being healed, they would stand and praise God. It happened once, twice, and continued until scores of people were standing. Miracles happened all around me. It was undeniable. Thoughts spun in my head; I couldn't understand what I was seeing.

> *Through that single event, God took me from the realm of theological argument and deposited me in the territory of divine experience.*

We returned home to Uppsala. I knew the experience had been real, but where did I fit into this? How could I touch God's power? I had seen more and understood less. My depression increased.

One day when Britta was at work and I was alone at home, Tolesa Gudina, an Ethiopian Lutheran pastor, came to visit. Tolesa lived closer to God than most men I know, and Jesus seemed to ooze from his every pore of his being. I had never seen him angry, never heard him argue with anyone. In many ways, he was the opposite of me. As he entered our little apartment, Tolesa sensed depression, and in a soft yet commanding voice said, "Get down on your knees."

I knelt.

He put his hands on my head and in a soft, gentle, barely audible whisper said, "Father, fill him with the Holy Spirit."

Before I could open my mouth to argue, something struck the top of my head. It felt like a bolt of lightning coursing through my body. A torrent of words in a strange language poured from my mouth, and I found myself shouting and worshiping Jesus in other tongues. Wave after wave of the glory of God came over me. I was caught up, worshiping Him who loved me and died for me. I felt Jesus in the room. I was filled—baptized with the Holy Ghost just as the Bible says! I felt the surge of Pentecostal power.

Every fiber of my being was ablaze, alive with electricity. That day I was baptized with Pentecostal fire, and I experienced it just as the disciples did on the Day of Pentecost (Acts 2). Through that single event, God took me from the realm of theological argument and deposited me in the territory of divine experience. It confirmed His Word in my life. Now I knew Jesus not only as my Savior, but also as the one who had baptized me with the Holy Ghost and with fire.

After this a number of our friends received the Holy Spirit in our little apartment, including our pastor's wife. The pastor, unfortunately, was not as enthusiastic about it as his wife. He summoned me to his office for a long talk, in which he clearly expressed his disapproval. The talk did not discourage Britta and me. We went on, and God continued to touch people. I recall one stunning occasion when we prayed for a friend to receive the Holy Spirit, and the power of God came down so strongly that the living room furniture shook for several minutes. At first I thought it was an earthquake, but I later learned that no quake was recorded. It was pure Holy Ghost.

Before I go on, I must say something more about Harry Greenwood, the first minister whom I saw move in the gifts of the Spirit and the power of God. In later years, I was privileged to get to know him and even minister alongside him. Brother Harry became one of my mentors, and I learned much from him. Some of things he taught me left indelible impressions on my life and ministry. He was a man of great joy, immense power, vast love, and broad humility. I was close to him until he went home to be with Jesus in 1988.

Two other things happened at about the same time that changed my life. The first had to do with my total deliverance from my bouts with depression. Although the baptism with the Holy Spirit had brought me into a new dimension of power and understanding of the Word of God, there were still times when I would feel down. These attacks of depressive thoughts that would come over me were mild and far less frequent. I felt only partially free.

One day, as I sat at home feeling sorry for myself for some now forgotten reason, God spoke to me and said, "Go to Elisabeth and lead her to Jesus." Elisabeth was the fiancée of a new Christian I knew.

"Me, Lord? I feel like I could do with some salvation myself." For most of my Christian life, I had been fixated on winning the lost, but the depression had taken the wind from my sails.

God spoke again, "Go."

I got up, changed, and took the bus to Elisabeth's place. I had called and asked Elisabeth's fiancé Kent to meet me there.

Two hours later Elisabeth had received Jesus. A sudden joy swept through me. Watching someone come to Christ filled me with unexpected enthusiasm. Words fail to describe the sensation, but I'll never forget it. It was the most powerful and complete cure for depression I had experienced. People had talked to me, counseled me, and tried to cast things out of me; nothing had helped. But this simple act of sharing the truth about Christ did for me what nothing else could do.

Obedience always leads to joy.

That was the last depression I experienced. That day I decided I would be the one to chase the devil instead of him chasing me. I was finally free.

The second thing that happened was that a friend who ran a Christian bookstore gave me a couple of books by Kenneth Hagin.

I had never heard of Reverend Hagin, but I took the books home and read them. I did more than read them; I devoured them. These books were different from anything I had read before—and I was an avid reader.

One was titled *What to Do When Faith Seems Weak and Victory Lost*. The book spoke to my situation and touched me deeply. I liked Kenneth Hagin's message of faith, his emphasis on trusting God's Word to change circumstances, and his commitment to move out of defeat and embrace victory. What set Hagin's books apart was the way they pushed me into studying the Bible. They offered concrete steps on how to trust God for miracles.

Kenneth Hagin's message had a profound impact on my thinking. My spiritual life was transformed, and I found myself moving in a new dimension of spiritual life.

I spent much time reading, studying the Word of God, praying, and worshiping. I sensed the surge of increasing faith in my inner being. The fire of God burned deep in my soul.

> *I understood God's promises were for today, and we did not have to make excuses for not seeing His power.*

Kenneth Hagin's books made me hungry for the Word of God. I was famished for biblical knowledge. I saw in the Bible things that I had never seen before. I understood God's promises were for today, and we did not have to make excuses for not seeing His power. We could see the same miracles and blessings today that we read of in the Word of God.

I was active in the church and the Swedish branch of Inter-Varsity Christian Fellowship and spent hours every day witnessing for Jesus on the streets. Now I began to pray for the sick and saw the same things manifested in my life that I saw in Harry Greenwood's meeting in Stockholm.

I must add here that at that time Kenneth Hagin was unknown in Sweden. That changed when his books were translated into Swedish. More and more people read his books and were changed. Kenneth Hagin became the hottest topic in churches. Some denominational leaders in Sweden, however, were not as enthusiastic about Brother Hagin's books. Many Christian leaders in Sweden went as far as denouncing him as a false prophet. They had never met the man, nor had they read his books, but they denounced him because of rumors and hearsay.

I would come to know Brother Hagin personally; in fact, I would go as far as to say that there was no one in Scandinavia who was as close to him as I was. Therefore, I can vouch for the man. He was truly a great man of God. Of all his qualities, that which made the most lasting impression on me was his humility. He was meek, lowly, and small in his own eyes. He walked in the love of God, neither criticizing others nor defending himself from those who attacked him. He loved Jesus and preached the Word of God, and I cannot even begin to tell of the things I learned from this great man of God.

Brother Hagin's books taught me the ABCs of God's promises and experiencing God's promises by faith. The power of God was so real now that I saw a constant stream of miracles and healings take place as I prayed for friends and others afflicted with illness. God used Kenneth Hagin's teachings to revolutionize my Christian life, bringing me into a new dimension of faith and power with God.

I was interested in obtaining more of Brother Hagin's books. I heard that one of the Lutheran chaplains at Uppsala University was going to the United States to attend one of Brother Hagin's seminars in Tulsa, Oklahoma. This chaplain's name was Ulf Ekman, and he was the brother-in-law of my friend who ran the Christian bookstore. I had never met him, but I was so eager for more of Hagin's books that I found his phone number and called him to ask if he would purchase books for me.

Ulf Ekman came back from America with a large number of Brother Hagin's books for me. I went to him to get the books, and when I offered to pay for them, he refused to accept the money, saying that they were a gift. Although we attended the same church, this was the first time I had met him.

One day Ulf and I sat down for coffee after a Sunday morning service. As we spoke, he asked me, "Do you have a friend, a brother, whom you can talk to about the deeper things of God?"

"No," I admitted.

"Then I will be that friend and brother," he replied.

From then on Ulf and I were inseparable. He became my closest friend, brother, and mentor. We met almost daily, praying and ministering together. We used to take long walks in the woods sharing our dreams and talking about the future when we would travel the world and do great things for God. We had a unique ministry together, standing side by side, speaking out words of knowledge, calling people out and praying for them, and seeing them healed by God. Our love and unity were an example to those around us and to those who came to the meetings where we ministered. We also had fun spending Christmas together. Britta and I were part of the small prayer group that met at his home. God used Ulf in my life, influencing and shaping vital aspects of my faith.

Ulf and I were close, and I worked with him until years later. But then a sharp disagreement sent us different ways. It was sad and painful to leave someone who had been dearer to me than a brother, someone whom I loved so much. My break with Ulf was the most painful experience of my Christian life.

We did not see each other or even talk for years, but then God brought us together again. We had grown and matured, and I am thankful to God for restoring my relationship with Ulf. Since then we have spent time together on different occasions, and I have had the privilege of ministering in his church in Uppsala. Ulf Ekman was, and remains to this day, a man greatly used of God.

His detractors point out his faults, but then who is without fault? I know that Ulf is not perfect, but then neither am I nor anybody else I know. Thank God that He chooses to look beyond our faults and to see us in Jesus. If He did not, then who could stand before Him?

About Ulf, all I can say is that I am happy to be able to look at Ulf today as a dear brother and a friend.

Chapter 17

SIGNS AND WONDERS

*I*HAD BEEN IN full-time ministry since shortly after I received Christ. Now I had been in Sweden for a couple of years, and we were doing ministry work when we could. Britta and I worked part time to support ourselves, and the rest of our time went into God's work. Nothing mattered more to us. We had no other interests except the work of the gospel.

The desire to return to full-time ministry burned in my heart. Several times I had been informed that every ministry in Sweden ran under the banners of the various denominations in the country and there was no opportunity for ministry outside those organizations. The fact there were no nondenominational churches in the entire country only proved the point. I was advised that the only way for me to be a part of denominational ministry was to attend one of their seminaries for three years. Then I would be accepted as a full-time minister. I dreaded the thought, because for me a "seminary" was synonymous with "cemetery." Education does have its virtues, but it is ultimately God, and not seminaries, that makes us men and women of God.

> *When I saw a person on the street with*
> *crutches, I would approach the hapless*
> *man, pray for him, and then try to snatch*
> *his crutches away.*

It seemed that I did not have much choice, so Britta and I visited two of the most reputable institutions in Sweden. I also took a closer look at the graduates they were producing and could not help but notice their lack of faith and lack of spiritual power. I did not want to end up in a similar condition, so I said, "No, thanks." It struck me that in some of these institutions, doubting the Word of God was lauded as a positive trait and a sign of higher learning and maturity. Simple childlike faith was considered naïve or stupid.

Rather than go to a seminary where they would suck the faith out of me, I decided to wait upon the Lord. I thought that if He wanted me to wait longer before entering full-time ministry again, then I would further my general education. I could then get a better job and continue to serve God part time. Not being one who pushed doors open for himself, I decided that the Lord would have His way with me as He pleased and in His own time. Being reasonably proficient in preparing and cooking different kinds of foods, I applied for training to become a restaurant chef and was accepted. I toyed with the idea of owning a nice French restaurant some day while doing ministry in my spare time. This was the summer of 1980.

I was waiting for the chefs' course to start in the fall, when unexpectedly, Ulf Ekman asked me if I would like to work with him as a full-time evangelist. The catch was that they could not give me a salary, and we would have to trust God for our needs. I sought the Lord about this and received a clear assurance from Him that this was His will. The job was full time, but there was no salary or benefits. But so what? The greatest reward of ministry is not remuneration but the privilege of serving. This was God's desire for me, and Britta and I knew He would provide.

We took this step of faith and dove headlong into the job, trusting the Lord to meet our needs. God responded by showing Himself faithful in every way.

God's healing power continued to fascinate me. I was so enthusiastic that I would descend upon sick people whenever I saw them. Crutches were my specialty and drew me like a magnet. When I saw a person on the street with crutches, I would approach the hapless man, pray for him, and then try to snatch his crutches away. That the man was a total stranger made no difference to me.

During those days of street ministry, I not only saw many people healed but also saw many who weren't. It was when people weren't healed that I learned some hard and valuable lessons. I was sincere in everything I did, but I was often unwise. At times I could be abrasive and arrogant in the way I dealt with people.

One event opened my eyes to my haughtiness. During a service at our Lutheran church, a girl who worked as a nurse at the local hospital stood and asked the congregation to pray for a little girl in the hospital who was dying of cancer. As the congregation began to mumble their prayers, I shot out of my seat. Britta, fearing what would come next, grabbed my arm and tried to pull me back down. I elbowed her objections away, left the pew, and marched up to the platform.

"I shall go to the hospital and lay my hands upon her," I proclaimed, "and she shall be healed." I quoted some scripture to boost my claim and went back to my seat.

The congregation sat in silence, stunned by my words. It didn't matter to me. I knew I was right.

The hospital was only two miles from the Christian bookshop I used as a base for ministry. The next day, Ulf Ekman and

I walked—no, marched—to the medical center armed with our Bibles and a bottle of oil for anointing. As we walked, we shouted in tongues and broadcast our great faith loudly for all to hear.

At the hospital, we found the afflicted girl's room. Inside, weeping parents waited for the inevitable. I boldly announced that she would be healed. We then prayed for the girl and anointed her with oil. After I returned home, I picked up the phone and called everybody I knew, telling them that the girl had been healed.

She died the next day.

> *Missing the mark doctrinally reveals a lack of knowledge, but pride and arrogance reveal something more serious—a lack of character.*

My heart sank when I heard the news. I was shaken beyond words. I had been so bold in my home church telling people, whom I considered skeptics and doubters, that the cancer-ridden girl would be healed. I had no doubt about the situation. For me her healing was a fact yet to happen.

But she died anyway. I had lost face before the whole church. I felt defeated and ashamed. In my despair, I sought the Lord. God can be brutally honest. As I prayed, He made clear to me some painful lessons.

First, I had more enthusiasm than faith. It was a hard thing to hear. Faith produces enthusiasm, but mere enthusiasm is not necessarily evidence of faith.

Second, I had to face the scorching truth: I had been more interested in seeing the girl healed so that I could brag, "God used me to heal someone from cancer," than by a genuine compassion for the girl. I did not care for the girl. All I wanted was another healing testimony under my belt, another feather in my hat.

Third, I had become a proud and arrogant man. I had

announced her impeding healing with flamboyance and pride, emphasizing my ability to pray for the sick, rather than proclaiming the healing power and compassion of Jesus.

God dealt strongly with me about this. I was humbled as I realized how wrong I had been in my attitudes and actions. The real danger in this had been my inability to see my faults and misplaced values. I had stood upon God's infallible Word as much as I could in the light of what I knew, but I had been blind to my own arrogance. This was hard to swallow, and I felt miserable. Out of that misery, the Lord saved my life by making my faults clear to me.

Humbled, broken, and crushed, I repented.

The Lord said to me, "Let God be true, but every man a liar" (Rom. 3:4). This meant that I could choose to base what I believed either upon God's Word alone or upon a combination of my experiences with a small amount of God's Word sprinkled in. I chose to believe God's Word in its entirety.

Jesus is and remains the healer, not me. Even if people are not healed, it does not change the fact that Jesus had borne upon Himself all the diseases of mankind. No matter what happens, Jesus Christ is always a healer.

We are not perfect, our preaching is not perfect, our faith is not perfect, but Jesus and God's Word are perfect. The good thing is that as we believe His Word and walk with Him, He causes us to grow and become more like Him. But it is often in the stinging rebukes from God that we learn the greatest lessons in life.

It was a painful lesson, but I learned it.

God corrected me in many of the attitudes and the injuries I had caused those to whom I had been called to minister. The Lord led me to approach each person and apologize. I also stood before the church and apologized for my arrogance. I had no excuse for being so un-Christlike in my behavior. Missing the mark doctrinally reveals a lack of knowledge, but pride and arrogance reveal something more serious—a lack of character. The first is easy to correct. The second deals with the heart and is a much deeper issue.

I discovered something interesting: whenever I apologized and made things right with those I hurt, God would take me one step higher on my spiritual journey. Those who refuse to humble themselves tread water the rest of their lives, never growing in God's grace or in ministry.

I learned at an early stage what terrible abominations pride and arrogance are to God. Even today, I find it difficult to sit and listen to preachers who preach with an air of superiority as if they are better than others. Jesus does not approach us from above shooting down at us. He comes down to our level, extending to us His mercy and loving us just as we are. From there He builds us up.

> And one of the elders saith unto me, Weep not: behold, the Lion of the tribe of Judah, the Root of David, hath prevailed to open the book, and to loose the seven seals thereof. And I beheld, and, lo, in the midst of the throne and of the four beasts, and in the midst of the elders, stood a Lamb as it had been slain.
>
> —REVELATION 5:5–6

The apostle John expected a conquering lion, but when he looked, he saw a lamb that had been slain. Jesus, who is a lion in His victory over Satan, is a meek lamb when He meets us. It is only through our meekness and brokenness that we can be lions in God.

Real strength is in brokenness and in meekness before God and before man. True spiritual strength is not in the might of the human flesh but in the power of God.

I increased my witnessing and was privileged to see many people receive Christ. God also began to work amazing healings and miracles. Working under Ulf Ekman in SESG, the Swedish branch of InterVarsity Christian Fellowship, I saw many university students and other people surrendering their lives to Jesus. Uppsala University was a stronghold of worldly humanism and intellectualism, but the Spirit of God pierced through the darkness into the hearts and minds of many. Many backsliders also rededicated their lives. The incurably sick were healed, and people tormented by demons were freed. It was wonderful to be where God was working so powerfully.

> **The first night more than forty people received the Holy Ghost; among them was the pastor who was literally knocked unconscious by the power of God.**

I then read another book by Kenneth Hagin: *The Name of Jesus.* This book enlightened my heart about that name that is above every name. I caught a glimpse of the power, the majesty of that worthy name, Jesus. It was as if the Lord had opened my eyes to a whole new dimension of His power. It was another life-changing revelation. I learned that the very mention of Jesus' name could cause sickness, diseases, and demons to flee. So great is the power of that name that the human mind cannot fully comprehend it.

Around this time I preached for the first time in a Lutheran church in Angelholm, Sweden. The first night more than forty people received the Holy Ghost; among them was the pastor who was literally knocked unconscious by the power of God. When he came to, he spoke in tongues incessantly until the next morning. Many were healed from diseases, causing some to mistakenly assume that I was some kind of hotshot "healing evangelist." These people, in their excitement, contacted a couple they knew in Helsingborg, about twenty-five miles away. This couple had a son who could not walk. They were wealthy people and had taken their little son to doctors in different countries. The physicians concluded that he was only the third known case in the whole world with that particular kind of infirmity and that there was nothing medical science could do to cure him. Medical researchers in Sweden, Denmark, and France were working to find some treatment for the boy. Man could do nothing, but we have a God for whom nothing is impossible. The Bible declares, "The things which are impossible with men are possible with God" (Luke 18:27).

The boy's mother came to the meeting with her son, and when I began to pray for the sick, she brought him to me for prayer. Everybody was watching. I didn't know what to do. I had never prayed for someone with such debilitating paralysis. What I did know, however, was the wonderful power in the name of Jesus that Brother Hagin's book had burned in my heart.

I prayed for the little boy with all my heart; I prayed in the mighty name of my Jesus. In a miraculous four-day process, God healed the boy. First, he was able to rise and walk a few steps, but then the paralysis would return. The next day, he walked a few steps further. His mother called me each day, encouraged but worried about the returning paralysis.

"Don't focus on the circumstance," I told her. "Praise God each day."

On the fourth day he walked with no return of the disease. When last I saw him, he was jumping and running like any other healthy child his age. The healing was complete.

Chapter 18

FURTHER TRAINING

⌒

KENNETH HAGIN HAS a Bible school in America where he trains ministers: Rhema Bible Training Center, in Broken Arrow, Oklahoma. Britta and I wanted to attend this school so that we could learn more about the Bible and ministry. In the summer of 1981 we traveled to America, excited about taking another step in our journey of faith.

The school has produced many powerful ministers of the gospel. One example is Ray McCauley of South Africa. Ray was runner-up in the Mr. Universe bodybuilding contest and a friend of Arnold Schwarzenegger. Ray graduated from Rhema and, upon his return home, started a powerful work that has shaken the nation of South Africa. He was one of the instruments God used in the peaceful process of reconciliation among the races in that heavily divided nation and in the peaceful exchange of power between the white minority apartheid government and the multiracial government headed by Nelson Mandela.

When fighting broke out in Rwanda and the world looked to President Mandela to bring peace to that nation, President Mandela asked Ray McCauley to represent him. Mandela even asked

Ray to be part of his cabinet, but Ray replied, "I am honored, Mr. President, but I can serve my country far better as a pastor." The thirty-thousand-member Rhema Bible Church that Ray McCauley pastors was started in the living room of Ray's father. Ray McCauley, by his message and by being a brother to me, has had a great influence on my life and ministry.

Getting to Rhema was not easy. Twice they turned down our application, but finally they accepted us—perhaps because we kept bombarding them with applications, using different avenues to get our applications in. The reason we were refused initially was that Rhema, in those days, could not help with student visas. We had to get the visas some other way.

The famous American Charismatic minister Harald Bredesen was visiting Sweden. He came to Uppsala for ministry and heard of our situation. He called a professor friend at Oral Roberts University in Tulsa, asking for help on our behalf. This professor, in turn, spoke to ORU graduate Billy Joe Daugherty, pastor of Victory Christian Center in Tulsa, who gave us a letter that would help the Ekmans and us get U.S. visas.

That I was given a U.S. visa was a real miracle because I, as a "stateless refugee," did not hold a proper passport. I carried a Swedish-issued, United Nations Geneva Convention Travel Document for Refugees, a *Passeport L'Etranger*. It made clear that I was not a Swedish subject. It is difficult to travel anywhere on this document, so the fact that I was given a three-month U.S. visa was a reason to rejoice.

Another miracle occurred upon our arrival at JFK Airport in New York. U.S. immigration extended my visa to six months. Later that extension would be further increased to allow us to finish our year of studies. This is unheard of, because U.S. immigration never grants extensions on these kinds of visas, but we prayed and our prayers were answered. Still, it was not an easy process. We went to the INS office in Oklahoma City, where we were ushered from one hard-nosed government employee to the next, and finally ended up in the office of the top official, who promised to look at our case.

"You have already received an extension given to you at JFK, and you want an additional extension?" He squinted at our documents.

"Yes, sir."

"Why?" It was a blunt question. "It is impossible. Two extensions are not allowed."

"We are attending a Bible school to further our education," I explained. "The extension will allow us to finish the full year of courses."

"Bible school?" He looked up and stared into my eyes, as if by doing so he could determine if I was lying.

I explained about the Rhema Bible Training Center.

He continued to stare, then released a wide, toothy grin. "I am with the Assemblies of God, and I respect Reverend Hagin's ministry. I know how important this is for you if you are going to serve the Lord. I am glad to be of service to you. God bless you."

We were on our way.

Harald Bredesen was an extraordinary man, always happy, always encouraging, and always sharing his faith. Love flowed from him like water from tap. Once he visited our tiny apartment to have dinner with us. It was a great privilege for us to receive a visit from such a distinguished man of God. We had heard how Bredesen used to dine with royalty and with presidents, so we decided to cook a dinner fitting his lofty status. Reverend Bredesen was staying at Ulf's house, and we asked Ulf if his guest preferred any particular type of food. Ulf told us the man preferred salads.

Britta had put a nice tablecloth on the little table in our tiny kitchenette, and we sat down to dinner. We had prepared a couple of different dishes and a large bowl of salad. I was awed by Harald

Bredesen's presence and summoned forth my best table manners, British-style, learned at the army officers' mess. Both Britta and I were tense and formal.

> *I had learned one of life's great lessons: to be real, whether among royalty or commoners, and to be yourself, free as a child of God.*

Everything went fine until the end of the meal when Harald Bredesen suddenly asked, "Does anybody want any more salad?" pointing to the large salad bowl on the table. Upon hearing that nobody wanted any more salad, he took the large salad bowl and proceeded to eat directly from it. Our tension melted, and we burst out laughing.

Harald Bredesen was "real," and I had learned one of life's great lessons: to be real, whether among royalty or commoners, and to be yourself, free as a child of God. I put this to the test years later when I was asked to minister at the home of the president of Malawi. I showed up in my jogging suit and sneakers and was received into His Excellency's home like a prophet of God.

There were five of us from Sweden attending Rhema. Ulf Ekman and his family were also part of this group. We were the first Swedes, actually the first ever group to come from overseas to attend the school. We considered it a privilege to sit under the powerful and anointed ministry of Kenneth Hagin. Our lives were transformed as we listened to the Word of God and watched the Holy Spirit move. Britta earned good grades. I, on the other hand, had never been academically inclined and found the study difficult. My dear wife pushed me on, and I made good grades in all the subjects.

For Britta and me, Rhema was a year of blessing and transformation. We went with little money and no promise of financial support; still we never advertised our material needs. We put the Word of God to the test and gave away money as we had never done before. It was amazing to see how God met our every need and blessed us daily.

We returned to Sweden and moved to the city of Linkoping, where we started a little Bible school with classes held twice a week. We had thirty-two excited students whom I taught. In addition to that, I traveled all over Sweden, preaching in different churches.

Chapter 11

INTO THE MISSIONS FIELD

⤳

/HE EMBER THAT burned in my heart for missions began to burn more deeply. God was fanning the flames. Almost immediately after my conversion I knew that I had been called to spread the gospel globally. My work with Operation Mobilization had verified that call. Now the hunger to go to foreign fields was insatiable. I prayed daily for open doors to other countries.

The answer came in July of 1983.

Poland still wore the mantle of a Communist nation, tightly tucked behind the Iron Curtain. Two Swedish friends and their wives planned to drive a van full of food to a Catholic youth camp in Tatry in the Carpathian Mountains of southern Poland. They invited me along, and I gladly accepted.

A brutal military government ruled Poland at the time, and the Catholic Church was the only successful force to stand against Communism. Baptists and Pentecostals, on the other hand, chose to collaborate with the Communists. I believe Poland was the only place in the Communist bloc where this was so. As a result, the Catholics were severely persecuted by the government. It was in this situation that God raised up an old priest, Father Blachnicki, as a voice for revival in the nation. He rose above the confines of religious traditions and began to preach the gospel of salvation. His message spread like wildfire, and people began to fill the churches. The success of his work caught the attention of the Polish government.

Blachnicki was deported to Germany. He died shortly after his arrival, never seeing his homeland of Poland again.

In spite of his absence, his Oasis Light and Life movement swept through the Catholic Church in Poland with a fresh wind of revival. Their message was threefold: (1) Experience new birth through Jesus, (2) read the Bible, and (3) fellowship with God through prayer. A strong Charismatic revival was also flowing through the Oasis movement, where spiritual gifts and the baptism with the Holy Spirit were emphasized.

Poland was under martial law, and the country suffered from an acute shortage of food and medical supplies. Christians from Western Europe were helping the Polish people with their needs by sending supplies. We were on such a mercy mission, and when we reached our Catholic friends, they opened their hearts to me and let me preach and minister to them.

The results still amaze me. Scores of people made decisions for Christ. There were healings and an outpouring of the Holy Spirit. Communism could restrict people's movement and their business, it could deprive them of freedom, but the Iron Curtain was no barrier to God.

We stayed in Poland for ten days (living on a pig farm), and at the end of our stay, I was asked to pray for a man who had been paralyzed in a traffic accident. He was unable to move from his chest down. I took the two Swedish brothers with me, and we went to the man's house.

I entered the room and saw the paralytic lying on his bed. The victim of a recent accident, the once fit and vital mechanic gazed back at me, his body trapped by a tragedy that robbed him of mobility. I could see the confusion, fear, and hopelessness in his eyes.

His wife stood beside the bed, a shell of a woman whose red, swollen eyes revealed the thousand tears she had shed. He was a picture of human suffering, a picture that forced me to realize how powerless man was in the face of such impossible odds.

I felt small. My mouth refused to form words. What could I do in a situation like this? But before I could surrender to despair, I felt something around me, filling the room. It was if a warm blanket had covered us all. It took a second for me to realize that the presence of Jesus had poured into the room and into me.

A verse of Scripture percolated to the top of my mind: "For where two or three are gathered together in my name, there am I in the midst of them" (Matt. 18:20).

Jesus was in our midst. I had no doubt of it.

I had no idea what to say, but words poured from mouth— words I hadn't planned, words not formed in my mind. It was as if someone else were speaking through me.

"Brother, fear not, because Jesus loves you, and God will raise you up."

It was a bold statement, a confident expression, but I didn't feel bold or confident. Still, I knew what I needed to do.

Taking the small jar of oil we had brought, I anointed him in the name of Jesus, prayed, and then stepped back from his bed.

For two minutes he lay still.

Words were not spoken.

We waited as seconds ticked by like hours.

He shifted under his blanket, then suddenly threw it aside. A moment later, he was out of bed and on his feet. With his hands uplifted he began praising God and walking around the room. One step followed another. He stood and moved with confidence and strength he should not have had.

The accident had broken several of his ribs, and the trauma had left his chest swollen. I placed my hands on his chest, and the swelling disappeared instantly.

> *Children born paralyzed walked for the*
> *first time; the twisted and deformed were*
> *made whole; the blind received sight; the*
> *deaf heard what they never heard before;*
> *tumors and cancers disappeared.*

What does a man do in the face of such a miracle? What is the appropriate behavior? For my companions and me, there existed only one choice: we dropped to our knees and wept with joy.

A crushing humility covered me. With the young girl with cancer, I had proclaimed with the greatest pride that I would pray for her and she would be healed. She died. Here, I knew that I had nothing to do with the healing of the man. The work had been done by Jesus—Jesus and no one else. He alone deserved glory and praise. I felt blessed to have seen the miracle.

God used that healing to open additional doors for me to preach in Poland. Miracles began to multiply. I returned to Poland many times and preached in Roman Catholic churches. Thousands came to listen, and thousands came to Christ. Jesus continued to touch the maimed, crippled, and broken. Children born paralyzed walked for the first time; the twisted and deformed were made whole; the blind received sight; the deaf heard what they never heard before; tumors and cancers disappeared. Much of this we recorded on videotape.

One healing held a special meaning for me. A young woman had been born with a deformity—her jaw was twisted and malformed. She had endured several surgeries. Doctors had attached metal plates to her jawbone with metal screws. She was a tortured soul.

She came to one of our meetings and stood in a crowd of seven thousand. God touched her where she stood. Later she told me what she felt.

"As I stood in the crowd with my eyes closed, and you began to pray, I felt the warm hands of God touch my jaw—moving, shaping, and forming—for about thirty seconds. Then I placed my hands to my jaw. It felt normal, perfectly shaped, no deformity, and the metal plates and screws that I had been able feel with my fingers were gone; they had disappeared."

In Pila, Poland, a mother carried her little girl to one of our meetings. The girl was crippled, her spine twisted and deformed. He legs folded inward and were pulled close to her chest, her knees almost touching her chin. She had been in that position all her life. She had never stood.

Thousands were at the meeting that evening, so many that I did not see the mother with her crippled daughter seated on the platform behind the huge altar table along with hundreds of other people. Near her was a team of twenty-seven people from Sweden and Norway who were traveling with me, and they were blessed to see the whole miracle as it happened.

I did not see the mother and child, but Jesus saw them and saw their faith. As I was praying over the crowd, I was interrupted by someone's scream. I turned and looked for the disturbance. People were crying and shouting as this little girl, let down to the floor by her mother, began to walk for the first time in her life.

> *The sight of God's greatness humbles a man. On my knees, I felt less significant than any other time in my life.*

The crowd went wild as they saw this. A wave of the glory of God rolled over the people. They began to throw aside their canes and crutches. Others were thrusting their crippled children to the platform, and those children began to walk.

When I saw the first girl walking, I reached out, took her

hand, and walked with her. After a few steps I suddenly realized the enormity of what God had done and what was happening all around me. It overwhelmed me, and I dropped to my knees. All I could say to the crowd was, "This is not the ministry of a man but the ministry of Jesus."

The sight of God's greatness humbles a man. On my knees, I felt less significant than any other time in my life. I needed a moment to myself—and a moment with God. I looked for a place to hide. I was next to the large altar, and I crawled under it, curled up in a corner, and sobbed like a child. The spiritual power was so intense I was certain I was about to die. I understood how Isaiah felt when he had his vision of God on His throne. The great prophet said, "Woe is me! for I am undone" (Isa. 6:5). It's an old phrase that means, "Woe is me, for I am about to die." Isaiah did not believe he would survive the vision. I was sure I wouldn't survive the night.

I did not weep because I thought death was near. I welcomed heaven. I wept because I was overcome with the purity and power of God's presence.

Under that altar, surrounded by the tumult of joy, praise, and astonishment, Jesus spoke to me. "You have seen nothing yet. Get back up before the people."

I crawled from under the altar. The Holy Spirit was pouring through the place like a tsunami of mercy and glory. There was such an outbreak of miracles. Multitudes were healed as the Holy Spirit moved over the crowd. A half dozen crippled boys walked up on the platform, placed there by their parents who had carried them forward. No one had touched them. God restored them the moment they were put on the platform. A weeping and shouting mass of humanity pressed forward, begging me to pray for them. They were crushing me against the solid altar table.

I stripped off my jacket and tossed it into the crowd. "The power of God is upon my jacket," I shouted.

The healing virtue of the Lord Jesus was so powerful upon

my jacket as it was being passed around through the crowd that people were being healed the instant they touched the jacket.

I do not remember how the service ended, but when I returned to Pila the following year, the priest of that church told me that miracles continued for three months after that meeting. People, he said, would line up daily bringing their canes and crutches, artificial legs, braces, spectacles, and hearing aids, testifying about what God had done for them. Today the thought of all God did in Pila still drives me to praise and prayer.

The above are just two examples of the many miracles that the Lord did in Poland. We saw tens of thousands come to Jesus and thousands of healings.

I noted that the Catholics showed an amazing reverence for the cross and for the blood of Jesus. They also displayed faith to receive miracles. On one occasion I was invited to Poland by Interland, a Swedish media company that cooperated with Polish National Television. They wanted to produce a TV documentary about miracles and had organized the meetings in a large Catholic church in Gdynia, Poland.

More than twelve thousand people showed up, eight thousand inside the building with four thousand outside. I preached about the blood of Jesus. One of Poland's main anchorwomen who was participating in the program and interviewing me broke down and wept, seeking the Savior. Thousands were saved, and outstanding miracles took place in large numbers. The TV crew chief wept as God touched and healed her while she stood directing her crew. They took down the names and addresses of ninety people who had received the most outstanding miracles. They visited these people in their homes three to six months after the meetings. Nothing had changed. Each person healed had remained healthy. Polish TV then made a seventy-minute miracle-packed documentary on these services called *The Crusade* and telecast it on prime time. They estimate seventeen million viewers watched the program the first time it aired. So many viewers called the TV station following the program that the station's telephone exchange broke down. The program was re-telecast twice soon after.

Such is the power and impact of what the apostle Paul called "the glorious gospel of the Lord Jesus."

Chapter 20

TO THE ENDS OF THE EARTH

FROM HUMBLE BEGINNINGS, preaching in small groups in Catholic churches in Poland, God has taken us to many nations, on five continents, proclaiming the gospel of our Lord Jesus Christ to those who have never heard it.

Wherever we preach the gospel, we see entire towns shaken by the power of God. Thousands receive Jesus. Criminals give up knives, knuckle dusters, clubs, and other weapons. They throw away stolen goods, rolls of ill-gotten money, and drugs. Others toss away charms and fetishes used in witchcraft. Often the police come out to see the weapons, stolen goods, and drugs that people have thrown away to be burned.

Crime rates plummet. New churches are born. Existing churches experience dramatic growth.

In two countries in southern Africa, police chiefs have said to me, "We have noted that wherever you hold a crusade, the crime rates always go down."

During political disturbances in Zimbabwe, violent mobs ran the streets, killing, burning, and looting. The government imposed a ban on all public gatherings. One local police chief, however, wanted us to hold a crusade because he knew that the gospel would calm things down. We came in, held a crusade, and peace settled on that city.

In Malawi, when I was between two major crusades, I had the opportunity to preach in a little village. About five hundred people turned out, and I delivered my sermon while standing under a tree. As I was about to close the meeting, the voice of God came to me. "There is a woman here who has a mentally retarded child at home. The child was born with brain damage. Pray for her, and I will heal her."

"Lord, I don't have the faith for this—"

"I did not ask you if you had the faith. I have the faith. You just do as I say."

One touch of God is more powerful than years of human effort.

I asked whether there was such a woman in the crowd. There was, and she came forward weeping. I prayed over a cloth that she could place on her child. She went home and placed the cloth on the child when she put her to bed that night. The next morning the child woke up healed and normal. Even the physical features often seen on a retarded child had disappeared. God had done it. The news of this miracle spread through the district. So many gave their lives to Jesus as a result that five new churches came into existence almost overnight.

My ministry is based on the knowledge that God can do anything. It takes just a touch of God's power to move a multitude. One touch of God is more powerful than years of human effort.

During the turbulent last years of apartheid in South Africa, violence raged everywhere. A Swedish missionary suggested that we hold a crusade in eSikhawini, which at that time was one of the most violence-torn towns in KwaZulu, in the Natal province of South Africa. People died daily on the streets, a result of political violence between elements of the Zulu-dominated Inkhata and the ANC parties.

My Africa team moved from our base in Harare, Zimbabwe, in order to prepare for the crusade. White South Africans in the nearby town of Empangeni thought that my Swedish team members were crazy even to go into eSikhawini, let alone hold a crusade there. The violent political activists who were doing the killing threatened my team, but we went nonetheless, knowing that "greater is he that is in you, than he that is in the world" (1 John 4:4).

The crusade started with only three hundred attending the first night. We were told that, for months, people dared not step out of their homes after dark because of the fear of violence. That first night we saw the leading *sangoma*, or witch, of eSikhawini give her life to Jesus. The second night there were seven hundred in attendance, and we saw God touch many people, including an event I will never forget.

A paralyzed boy was there. But his paralysis did not stem from injury or birth defect; his was an affliction of witchcraft. When I first saw him, he was stiff as a board, unable to move, speak, hear, or respond in any way. His eyes stared vacantly into space. His face had no expression. He had been in this state for a few years. The family said it was the result of a witchdoctor's curse.

As I was preaching that night, he stirred to life, stood, and asked his mother, "Mama, where are we?" He was set free, delivered by God's power.

This miracle touched the whole town and opened the gates of God's power in eSikhawini. The grip of fear was broken, and people came out by the thousands. Close to one-third of the population came to one of the services. Whites and Indians from the neighboring towns of Richards Bay and Empangeni came out to hear the Word of God. Thousands responded to the call for salvation. The gospel had broken through in eSikhawini.

The week we were there, and for weeks afterward, not a single killing occurred. The townspeople, for the first time in months, ventured outdoors after dark.

In Rosario, Argentina, a large multitude gathered to hear the gospel. Tens of thousands came to Jesus each night, and thousands received the baptism with the Holy Ghost. The Holy Ghost fell so powerfully that there were those who started praising God in other tongues in the evening crusade and didn't stop until the next morning. Large numbers of deaf, mute, blind, and crippled individuals were healed; arms and legs grew out by up to eight inches, and tumors and cancers vanished.

In one case, a woman paralyzed for sixteen years rose from her wheelchair and walked just as I read to the crowd the Bible passage from which I would preach. It was Psalm 103:2–3, "Bless the LORD, O my soul, and forget not all his benefits: Who forgiveth all thine iniquities; who healeth all thy diseases."

As I read these words, the crowd began to shout, and I saw what God had done. On another night seventy-nine blind people received their sight. Never in my life had I imagined seeing anything like that.

Every evening, as I would get up to preach, large numbers of demon-possessed people would fall to the ground screaming. They would then be carried to the large deliverance tent, where fifty people worked full time casting devils out of the people.

The gates of hell were shaken, thousands gave their lives to Jesus, and I'm certain the devil had a nervous breakdown.

Rosario was a center for witchcraft. Hundreds of practitioners were delivered from the powers of darkness. Witches and warlocks who came to the crusade were set free.

Some witches, angry at what was happening, hired a man to kill me. He came to the crusade and stood among the people waiting for an opportune moment. As I preached about Jesus, this man fell on the ground, shouting, "I have been sent to kill Christopher Alam. Tell him to stop preaching." He too was delivered and set free.

For twelve days, God shook Rosario, showing His mighty power to save, heal, and deliver. The gates of hell were shaken, thousands gave their lives to Jesus, and I'm certain the devil had a nervous breakdown.

After a crusade in Blantyre, Malawi, people would bring the sick and the infirm to the field where the crusade was held weeks before. As they set foot on the ground, they would be healed. How could this be? I believe that the gospel of Jesus Christ is the most powerful force in the universe. The apostle Paul cried out that the gospel "is the power of God...to everyone that believeth" (Rom. 1:16). Wherever the gospel is preached under the anointing of the Holy Spirit, wherever the precious blood of Jesus is proclaimed in all its power, the power of God is revealed. It is beyond human comprehension. The omnipotent work of the Holy Spirit, which so filled Peter that it was even in his shadow (Acts 5:15), is able to permeate even the soil upon which the gospel is preached. Such is the power of this life-giving gospel of Jesus.

As we see and hear of these things, it would be a fatal mistake to associate God's glory with me or any other person of God. This gospel is far greater than any preacher, and it is certainly far greater than me. It is true that God uses man, but then what would man be without Jesus? Without Jesus, even the best of us is nothing. The apostle Paul said about the power and glory of God that dwells in us, "But we have this treasure in earthen vessels, that the excellency of the power may be of God, and not of us" (2 Cor. 4:7).

We are vessels for the Master's use, and it doesn't matter if the vessel is of gold or silver, but rather what is the treasure in the vessel. The vessel itself is of little value, but what makes it special is the treasure that is within. We are earthen vessels, easily cracked or broken, but the treasure we carry inside because of God's grace upon us is His glory. It is *all* His and not ours.

> **The omnipotent work of the Holy Spirit, which so filled Peter that it was even in his shadow, is able to permeate even the soil upon which the gospel is preached.**

Two thousand years ago, Jesus made a special trip to Jerusalem riding into the city on a borrowed donkey. What mattered that day was not the pedigree of the donkey, but the nature of Jesus who rode upon it. In my case, I know God does not use me because of who I am but in spite of who I am. Without Jesus we are all big zeroes. I am no different. Wherever the gospel of Christ is proclaimed, there Jesus is, and He shows His power and compassion as He did when He walked on this earth two thousand years ago.

Chapter 21

LOOKING BACK

◡◠

I WAS BORN A Muslim, having no knowledge of Jesus, the Son of God and Savior of all mankind. He saved me from a life filled with sin, hurt, fear, and hatred. It felt as if I had lived and died a thousand times during the first twenty-one years of my life. The day Jesus came into my heart was the beginning of a new life; old things passed away, and I was born into a new, fulfilling life.

People ask me, "What about your father?" After I escaped Pakistan, I regularly wrote letters to my father. I did this for seven years, but he refused write back. Later I would learn that he would tear my letters up unread and throw them away. Whenever my name came up, he told people I was dead.

Years later, my father relocated to Bangladesh. My friend Ulf Ekman traveled to the country, and while he was there, he searched for and found my father. He paid a visit. My father received him, and Ulf told him about my new and firstborn son, Immanuel, his first grandchild. Somehow the thought of a grandchild softened his heart. He was immensely proud that it was a boy. Still, he refused to send a message or even a greeting to me. He did, however, send 500 pounds sterling to Immanuel.

In 1984, I flew down to see him unannounced and stood outside the gates of his house. I rang the bell. A servant came and answered, and I asked to see my father. He came out to the door. He had changed. Age had marred his face, his hair was white, and he stooped slightly. His military bearing, however, was still in place.

Moments ticked by as we looked at each other. Tension spanned the short distance between us. I watched his eyes soften and his shoulders dip. Without a word, we fell into each other's arms. Tears ran freely. It was a time of healing and restoration.

> ### *The peace of God filled the room, and my father began to sob.*

I visited him many times until he died. I was on a crusade in Zimbabwe when I received the news that my father was seriously ill and not expected to live. On one hand, I wanted to be with him during his last moments, but I could not do so. As the oldest son, I was expected to lead the Muslim prayers, rites, and rituals that accompanied a funeral. Refusing to do so would be a serious insult to his memory. Because of this I decided it was best not to go. It was a difficult decision, but I felt that I had no choice. Instead, I requested a pastor friend in Bangladesh to visit my father in the hospital.

This pastor made the visit. When he entered my father's room he walked to his bedside and introduced himself as a "Christian pastor and friend of your son." My father was conscious and had some strength left. He took the pastor's hand and pulled him down to sit on the bed. The pastor then began to pray in the name of Jesus, and as he prayed, something amazing happened. The peace of God filled the room, and my father began to sob. Tears streamed down his face, and he wept for a long time. The pastor kept praying, and my father held his hand tightly and would not let him go. God was doing something in my father's heart.

A few days later my father died. They buried him between the graves of his parents.

Not long after, I flew to Bangladesh to visit my father's grave. I stood in the cemetery, my heart a cauldron of emotion. Sorrow and pain boiled within me as I thought of our fractured, painful relationship—so many years, so many wounds, so many things unspoken. I felt like a fractured teapot that had been pieced back together—whole but with cracks still visible. Childhood memories swarmed in my head, the good recollections followed by the painful.

What could be said now? What words could be uttered that would make a difference to our history? Apologies? Sentences spewed in wrath? There were no words, just throbbing scars.

I looked up. The sky wore its deep blue, its face decorated with a few wisps of cloud. I prayed. And prayed.

There at the graveside, with my feet inches from my father's final resting place but my mind still anchored to a stormy past, the Holy Spirit paid a visit. A great peace covered my soul as the cerulean sky covered the day.

Even at a graveside, God remained good.

The Spirit of God brought to my remembrance the way He had touched my father when my pastor friend prayed for him during his final hours. I felt a deep assurance in my heart that the Lord had put His hand upon my father just as He had put His hand upon me. In the end, we finally had something in common.

I laughed, and the sound of it brought relief to my soul. Praise followed the laughter. Even at a graveside, God remained good.

I left the cemetery and arranged a huge meal for hundreds of poor people. It was something Father did from time to time, and I could think of no better way to honor his name. I then visited my stepmother and her children and spent time with them assuring them of my love and that I harbored no resentment toward them. They could ask me for help if ever they needed anything. It turned out to be an unappreciated gesture.

Some weeks later I received a telephone call and learned that my stepmother was working behind my back, quietly filing an affidavit in the courts stating that she and her children were the sole surviving heirs of my father, mentioning nothing about my brother or me. She asked the court to release my father's property to her and to her children. He had left behind a huge bank account, a large house, housing and industrial lands, and a large farm. This was the procedure the family of a deceased person had to follow in order to initiate the distribution of the deceased's assets. As the oldest son, I was entitled by law to receive half of everything. My stepmother, however, wanted it all. Since I lived overseas, she hoped I would not learn of her actions. Thanks to the caller, I did.

The betrayal stung, and my first course of action was prayer. I went before the Lord seeking His wisdom. Some of my friends and relatives, even well-meaning minister friends, advised me to go to court and reclaim my inheritance. If I did so, the authorities would prosecute her for fraud, and she would be left penniless.

As I sought the Lord's direction, I reflected on all that I could do with the money. I had no personal savings. I could use the money to pay off my house and put my children through college. It was my inheritance after all. To us Arabs, things like birthright and inheritance mean a lot.

"Ask of me, and I shall give thee the heathen for thine inheritance, and the uttermost parts of the earth for thy possession." I heard these words from Psalm 2:8 in an audible voice when I was before the Lord lamenting what my stepmother had done. The Lord spoke to me telling me to let go and to allow my stepmother to have what she wanted. I was to walk away from it all. He would provide for my family and me; we would never lack anything, and

He would bless us with more than that which was stolen. The heathen would be my inheritance, and I would possess nations—not for me—but for Jesus.

"Ask of me, and I shall give thee the heathen for thine inheritance, and the uttermost parts of the earth for thy possession." The Lord repeated these words several times a day for weeks in a row. They burned in my heart. I understood what the Lord was saying, that the heathen were my inheritance, but...

The Lord said, "Don't you get it? I am not asking for your assent; I am saying, *ask of Me.*"

That got my attention.

"My people ask Me for money, cars, and houses because I said that I would give them whatsoever they asked for. They ask Me for all those things, but here is a place in my Word where I tell them *what* to ask for, and it is the one thing they never ask. *Ask Me* for the heathen as your inheritance, and see what I will do for you."

"Lord, I ask You for the heathen as my inheritance. I ask You for the nations."

The prayer released a pent-up reservoir of tears. It also brought a profound sense of relief. God had made my mind up for me.

A few weeks later, I was in one of the most closed nations on this earth (whose name I am not at liberty to mention), where there are few Christians, and those few are heavily persecuted. Preaching the gospel is forbidden. I had been visiting and ministering there for a couple of years, but this time I took a bold step of faith and held an open-air crusade. Thousands of people received Jesus, and God sent fire from heaven as multitudes were healed and delivered from demons. Even Buddhist monks came to receive Jesus. For the first time in the history of that nation, the gospel went out openly with power, and multitudes came to Jesus. On the last night, as I looked out over the sea of hands raised to God and the thousands of tear-streaked faces seeking the Savior, I again heard the voice of God.

"This is your inheritance; this is your possession. This is what

I will do through you."

I thanked God and rejoiced. This was priceless, of far greater value than the all the money and property that my father had left behind. My stepmother could keep it all. I wanted more of *this*.

> *Jesus has taken the land from the hand of Satan and has given it to us, God's people. It is our inheritance, our possession.*

Since that day we have seen the beginnings of revival in that nation. God has told me to plant five hundred new churches in that nation, of which, at the time of this writing, we have planted ninety. We have held crusades, and tens of thousands have come to Jesus. Many of them are preaching the gospel today. Innumerable and mind-boggling miracles have taken place, including the healing of people with AIDS and the dead being raised to life.* God gave me an open vision of a tidal wave of the blood of Jesus washing over that nation from the south to the north, and I am seeing it come to pass. Jesus has taken the land from the hand of Satan and has given it to us, God's people. It is our inheritance, our possession. All that God has promised is happening.

All glory to our Lord Jesus!

God has done a great work of restoration in my life. I was full of hate and did not know how to give or receive love. Today, I love people. I am filled with the love of Jesus "because the love of God is shed abroad in our hearts by the Holy Ghost which is given unto us" (Rom. 5:5).

Once I was an outcast, but I now belong to God's family. I have many brothers and sisters who love me, pray for my family, sup-

---

* One such case included a man who was carried to the crusade but died soon after arriving. Medical personnel checked him and pronounced him dead. We prayed and cried out to God. The power of God settled on the deceased, and God raised him back to life.

port us, and show their care in many ways.

Some years ago, Britta and I felt a desire to move our family to the United States. We prayed and waited for three years for the Lord to show us the right time and the place for us to move. America is a big place, but we wanted to relocate to a place where there was a church whose heartbeat and passion was to reach the world with the gospel of Jesus.

In 1992, Ray McCauley asked me if I would like to accompany him to Kenneth Hagin's 20th Camp Meeting in Tulsa, Oklahoma. I flew from Sweden to attend and was soon sitting in a crowd of more than ten thousand at the first night's service. I hardly knew anyone there, so I looked around until I found Reverend Jim Kaseman and his wife, Kathy, whom I had known for many years, and sat next to them. People milled about, looking for seats, talking.

I was tired, drowsy from jet lag, and fighting to keep my eyes open when I heard, "Christopher Alam, please come to the platform."

I stirred as I heard my name called over the public address system. I looked at the Kasemans.

"Go to the platform," Kathy Kaseman urged me. "They are calling you."

I made my way from my seat to the platform and asked the usher if there was a problem. He took me on stage and asked me to sit there next to Kenneth Hagin. Brother Hagin asked me to share in that evening's service.

I was so nervous that I had even forgotten to bring my Bible with me. I left it on my seat next to the Kasemans. I don't recall what I said that night, but I do remember the scripture I used: Leviticus 6:13—"The fire shall ever be burning upon the altar; it shall never go out."

One minister in the audience that night was Pastor Sam Smucker of The Worship Center, in Lancaster, Pennsylvania. A missionary from that church, Oliver Lindberg from Sweden, is one of my closest friends. Afterward Oliver introduced me to Pastor

Sam, and we had lunch together two days later.

During the course of our conversation, Pastor Sam invited me to preach in his church. It was a gracious invitation, one I considered for ten months.

In May 1993, I found myself preaching at The Worship Center. I was very impressed with Pastor Sam. Coming from an Amish background, he is one of the humblest men I have ever met. I saw his heart for the salvation of the lost. I witnessed how wonderful the people in his congregation were. They were humble, kind, and generous. Europeans perceive Americans as superficial, loud, rude, pushy, and arrogant. These people were certainly different. Furthermore, this church had a passion for foreign missions.

> *The lame walk, the blind see, the deaf hear, the mute speak, the dead rise, and twisted and deformed bodies are healed by the touch of Jesus. But the greatest miracle is watching the Father take a sinner and turn him into a child of God.*

In one service, as I preached about winning souls for Jesus and about laying down our lives for the gospel, I was surprised to see big tears rolling down Pastor Sam's cheeks. *This is the man I would like to have as my pastor. He knows the heart of God,* I thought to myself.

Those tears kindled in me a desire to move to Lancaster, Pennsylvania.

I then knew that this was the place for us. I did not want to express this to Pastor Sam, but I asked God to put it into his heart. I wanted the invitation to come from him.

A week passed before Pastor Sam offered to help us move to America. The Worship Center agreed to sponsor our move with the U.S. authorities. My friend Bill Lee, of Asheville, North Carolina, engaged one of the top immigration lawyers in the country to file our application for immigration.

We had heard horror stories about people waiting years for their applications to be processed. We prayed, and our papers moved at lightning speed. We had our "green cards" in four months. This included a five-week period when our papers were lost in the mail.

We moved to the United States of America on December 13, 1993. Ten years later, on January 14, 2004, we became citizens of the United States.

America is now our home.

I stand amazed at the goodness of God. Today, when I think of my past, it seems as though I am thinking about someone else. Jesus changes lives. In my twenty-two years as a Muslim, I never received a single answer to prayer. Allah never spoke to me, nor did I ever feel his presence in my life. He was a distant, silent god.

Coming to Jesus changed everything. The one and only true God, whom I never knew, the Father of the Lord Jesus Christ, received and embraced me. He became my Father, and I became His child. Today I hear His voice and know His presence. I am His child.

He not only saved me and carried me to victory through persecution, but He also healed me, baptized me with the Holy Ghost and with fire, and thrust me into the harvest field to bring the lost to Him. I have been all over the world and have seen millions of people come to Jesus. I have seen cities and nations shaken by the gospel. The lame walk, the blind see, the deaf hear, the mute speak, the dead rise, and twisted and deformed bodies are healed by the touch of Jesus. But the greatest miracle is watching the Father take a sinner and turn him into a child of God, cleansing him inside and out. Gone are the rags of sin and misery. Instead, God clothes us in sparkling white robes of righteousness.

Any sacrifice we make pales in comparison with what it cost Jesus to purchase our redemption. It is like holding a candle to the sun.

Some may say, "Brother, you suffered so much for the gospel; it cost you so much."

To them I say, "The real sacrifice was paid by Jesus to redeem us from our sins and diseases. Those tears and bloody sweat at Gethsemane; the brutal scourging at the whipping post; that cruel crown of thorns; the mocking, the spitting, and blows of the Roman soldiers; the pain, the loneliness, the shedding of the precious blood; and finally, His death upon the cross at Calvary. All because of His love for sinners—His love for us."

Any sacrifice we make pales in comparison with what it cost Him to purchase our redemption. It is like holding a candle to the sun.

Paul said, "But God forbid that I should glory, save in the cross of our Lord Jesus Christ, by whom the world is crucified unto me, and I unto the world" (Gal. 6:14). We would be fools to glory in ourselves or in what we think we have accomplished.

There were and are many others much better than me, but God reached down, saved me, and called me because of His own grace and purpose. I cannot yet comprehend the fullness of His love and power, but this one thing I know—that He has been good to me.

Let this testimony be for the glory of God, to Him alone, who is worthy to receive glory, honor, and praise for all that He has done.

> For God so loved the world, that he gave his only begotten Son, that whosoever believeth in him should not perish, but have everlasting life. For God sent not his Son into the

world to condemn the world; but that the world through him might be saved.

—JOHN 3:16–17

It is a wonderful life. I have received far more than I could ever deserve, and that is because of God's grace. I am most grateful to the Lord.

Chapter 22

LOOKING AHEAD

I AM NOW PART of God's mighty army, a force that is shaking the earth through the preaching of the gospel. We are pushing ahead with crusades in Africa, Asia, and in many other parts of the world.

I am privileged to be a child of God, and I am blessed to have a wonderful family and a team of anointed colaborers. They are precious people, and we stand together for Jesus. They work hard, laying down their lives for the gospel. Time is short, and Jesus is coming back to the earth soon. The harvest is plenteous, but the laborers are few. We have preached the gospel to millions, yet millions are still unreached.

My belief is God wants to bless us with all good things, spiritually and materially. The Bible says, "All things are yours." (See 1 Corinthians 3:21; Romans 8:32.) Yet the Bible also speaks of sacrifice, self-denial, and a willingness we should have to lay down our lives for Jesus. At times, God may call us to sacrifice so that others may have that which is more valuable than all things: salvation through Jesus Christ. We can sacrifice the gold of this world so that others may one day walk on heaven's golden streets. We do not know how much time we have left to finish the task the Lord has entrusted to us, but we continue on. The task is great, but the power and grace given to us is far greater. There is salvation, healing, and deliverance in rich abundance for all who believe.

We count the eternal destinies of the lost as far greater worth than our own lives. That is why Jesus died for us. He bore His cross for us. Now He calls us to take up our cross and walk with Him.

What will you do with your life? Will you say *yes* to the call of the Master? Will you follow Him? God will anoint you with the Holy Ghost and with fire.

Say, "Yes, Lord," to Jesus, and let Him send His fire to fall upon you, setting you ablaze for His kingdom and His glory. Let us arise together and win this world for Jesus. Let us live this life 100 percent for Jesus. If we are willing to die for Him, then we are fit to live for Him. It is all or nothing. It is by giving our all to Him that we enter into the fullness of God. So come on; let's love and serve Jesus with all our hearts.

> Put ye in the sickle, for the harvest is ripe…
>
> —Joel 3:13

Jesus is coming soon. Are you ready?

Epilogue

AN INVITATION TO YOU

I F THIS BOOK has touched your heart and you want to invite Jesus Christ into your heart to become your Lord and Savior, then please pray this simple prayer:

Father God, I come to You in the name of Your Son, Jesus Christ. Lord Jesus, I thank You for shedding Your precious blood upon the cross for me. I believe that You died for me and rose again. I believe that You are alive today. Jesus, I give You all my sin. Wash me in your precious blood; make my heart clean and white as snow. Come into my heart right now and be the Lord of my life. In Jesus' name, amen.

If you prayed this prayer, then you are now a child of God. You belong to God's great family.

Let me now tell you about the four steps to victory:

1. Read from the New Testament every day.

2. Pray to God, your heavenly Father. Prayer is talking to God just as a child talks to his or her father.

3. Tell others about what Jesus has done for you.

4. Begin to attend a good gospel-preaching church.

I advise you to contact the closest full gospel, Pentecostal, or Charismatic church. Tell them of your decision to follow Jesus. They will be glad to help and guide you.

You may also contact me at:

Dynamis World Ministries
(aka Christopher Alam Ministries International)
2384 New Holland Pike
Lancaster, PA 17601
Telephone: (717) 656–0362
Fax: (717) 390–0363
E-mail: dynamis-usa@pentecostalfire.com

Appendix

MY LITTLE "CONNECTION" WITH POPE
JOHN PAUL II AND WITH HISTORY

I LEFT RHEMA IN 1982. A year later, in June 1983, I went on my
first missions trip. It was a humanitarian mission to Poland.
I was asked to accompany a load of food supplies designated
for a teaching camp held by the Catholic Church for university
students and graduates from Krakow, Poland. Upon arriving, I
was given the opportunity to minister to the students. Every single unsaved person was saved. Many were baptized with the Holy
Ghost, and many were healed. On my last day there, God healed
a man who was paralyzed from the chest down. This miracle created a stir, and suddenly, the doors of the entire Catholic Church
in Poland were thrown open to me!

That night while ministering to the students for the last time,
the Holy Ghost came upon me like a heavy mantle, and I began to
weep and prophesy the words of the prophet Isaiah in Isaiah 54:

> Sing, O barren, thou that didst not bear; break forth into
> singing, and cry aloud, thou that didst not travail with child:
> for more are the children of the desolate than the children

of the married wife, saith the LORD. Enlarge the place of thy tent, and let them stretch forth the curtains of thine habitations: spare not, lengthen thy cords, and strengthen thy stakes; for thou shalt break forth on the right hand and on the left; and thy seed shall inherit the Gentiles, and make the desolate cities to be inhabited.

Fear not; for thou shalt not be ashamed: neither be thou confounded; for thou shalt not be put to shame: for thou shalt forget the shame of thy youth, and shalt not remember the reproach of thy widowhood any more. For thy Maker is thine husband; the LORD of hosts is his name; and thy Redeemer the Holy One of Israel; the God of the whole earth shall he be called.

For the LORD hath called thee as a woman forsaken and grieved in spirit, and a wife of youth, when thou wast refused, saith thy God. For a small moment have I forsaken thee; but with great mercies will I gather thee. In a little wrath I hid my face from thee for a moment; but with everlasting kindness will I have mercy on thee, saith the LORD thy Redeemer....

I recited the entire chapter. The students began to shout and rejoice; some fell on their knees and wept. They were shouting, "Poland shall be free! Communism shall fall! Hallelujah!" I wept tears of joy. I knew that this was a historic moment. The Lord had spoken, and great things were to happen in that nation. At that moment the Lord ignited within my heart a fiery passion to take the gospel to Poland. He put within my heart a supernatural love for the Polish people that I still carry today.

I had walked into a situation that I knew very little about prior to my first trip to the country. All I knew was that Poland was a Communist country, that she was in the grip of military rule, and that there was an acute shortage of food. Sweden, where I lived and was a citizen, was Poland's neighbor, and we wanted to help. That is why I went there. Little did I know that I had walked right into something that was part of God's plan for the nation and for the whole of Eastern Europe.

These students, graduates, and their leaders to whom I had ministered were from the University of Krakow in southern Poland. They were a group of two thousand firebrands who met every day at the large Dominican church in the city center. Pope John Paul II had been the bishop of Krakow just before he became pope. He loved to ski and walk in the Tatry Mountains, and he did so with these young people. He loved them, spent much time with them, and mentored them. He kept in close touch even after going to Rome as pope. Their leaders visited him often in Rome. These were the very people whom I had become close to and was working with to take the gospel to Poland.

Many people in America credit President Ronald Reagan and America's military might as being behind the fall of Communism. Those of us who lived in Europe and saw history unfold see it differently. Communism was actually overthrown by the oppressed people in Communist-ruled countries who yearned for freedom after decades of slavery. They rose and broke the chains that bound them. The uprising first started in Poland, spread to Romania, ignited East Germany, traveled to the rest of Eastern Europe, and finally to Russia itself.

The man who first ignited these flames of freedom was Pope John Paul II, who was Polish and wanted to see his beloved Poland free. Reagan did have a major part, but it was the pope who started it all. He went to Poland and stirred up the nation, preaching about freedom to huge crowds numbering in the millions. After that the pope went to see Gorbachev, and then advised Reagan to do so also. The Polish people rallied around the only institution that was strong enough to resist the Communists, and that institution was the Roman Catholic Church.

From this arose two groups who began the revolt against Communism. Both groups consisted of people who were close to John Paul II and looked to him for guidance and inspiration. One was the Solidarity Workers' Union, who influenced factory workers all over Poland, and the others were these firebrand students of the Light and Life movement who influenced students groups in universities and churches all over Poland. They spoke of freedom, and they preached that salvation through Jesus and the baptism with the Holy Spirit were for everybody.

These were the students and leaders with whom God had suddenly put me. They were at the forefront of the uprising that began in Poland and was to ultimately destroy the hold of Communism over Eastern Europe. They wanted me to come to Poland as much as possible and preach all over the nation. They believed that there was a deep intermeshing of the gospel message with the uprising against Communism. Just as the gospel brought spiritual freedom, the uprising would bring national freedom. The first would influence the latter as their dreams of national freedom were inspired by God—that it would come to pass without violence. That is why they wanted the gospel with demonstrations of the miracle-working power of Jesus Christ.

From 1983 on until Communism fell, I ministered in meetings with thousands of these students in groups and in large Catholic churches all over Poland. Tens of thousands of people would come to hear the gospel and receive Christ. The most amazing miracles that I have ever seen in my ministry happened in those meetings. Children whose bodies were crippled and twisted rose up and walked…blind eyes saw…people left their wheelchairs…creative miracles took place. The miracles are too many to number. The Catholic priests were hungry for the power of God and asked me to hold teaching seminars in seminaries and in monasteries. I also translated and distributed Brother Hagin's books and tapes all over Poland. Priests, monks, and nuns in seminaries, churches, and monasteries all over the nation were studying his materials. I was in Poland often during those years; after all, it was just south of Sweden where I lived. Because of my Swedish passport I could go into Poland easily, and as such, to the best of my knowledge, we were the only ones who did any major ministry in Poland during that time.

Government authorities were concerned about these meetings. The secret police followed me around, but they never touched me because they feared the power of God. There were times when they were thrown down forcefully to the ground by the power of God.

My friends who were close to Pope John Paul II reported to him about my meetings, and they would often tell me what he had said in response. At times they would bring me messages of appreciation and encouragement sent by the pope. I knew the pope loved Jesus and that he spoke in tongues (later corroborated by Reverend David DuPlessis's younger brother Reverend Justus DuPlessis, a Pentecostal pastor who was also close to the pope). Such news made all this more meaningful. I toyed with the idea of going to Rome to meet him, but I felt that there was no real purpose to it. Furthermore, there were those in our own circles who disliked Catholics and were upset that I ministered in Catholic churches, and I did not want to make things worse. I knew that there were teachings in the Catholic Church with which we did not agree, but then there were people there who truly loved Jesus; there were multitudes there that really needed Jesus and the gift of salvation that only He could give.

I kept up intense ministry in Poland, working alongside these anti-Communist leaders, both ministering to them and advising them on spiritual and other matters. Finally the time came when Communism fell and Poland was free. Polish National Television arranged a large crusade for me in the big cathedral in Gdansk. They then made a ninety-minute film on all the miracles they saw and aired it nationwide during prime time. That was my last big meeting. I had received "special grace" from the Lord for Poland until Communism fell, and now I felt that grace for that nation "lifted," and I began to focus on other places.

For all that the Lord did during those turbulent but exciting times, I give all glory to our Lord Jesus, because He alone is worthy. I played a tiny little part in history and am thankful for the grace that the Lord gave me for that time.

Giants have walked the face of this earth in our times—spiritual giants like Dad Hagin and others who were "giants" in other ways, people like Ronald Reagan, Mother Teresa, and Pope John Paul II. They set examples for future generations to follow. We live in times of great selfishness, and we do not see many spiritual or political leaders of the same greatness that we have in times past. Many seek their own, and their motives are all muddled. Let us pray for God's church and for the nations that God would once again raise up men and women of such selfless integrity as He did before.

Most of all, let us continue to preach this glorious gospel of our Lord Jesus until He returns. Maranatha!

ABOUT THE AUTHOR

CHRISTOPHER ALAM IS the founder and leader of Dynamis World Ministries, a worldwide missions organization. Dynamis World Ministries has offices, teams, and bases in the United States, Zimbabwe, Sweden, and in one of the most unreached nations of Southeast Asia.

Christopher Alam and his ministry hold large open-air gospel crusades reaching millions of people in difficult and unreached places. They plant churches; hold schools of ministry for pastors, evangelists, and leaders; translate and publish faith-building books; distribute Bibles; and also run a training center for church planters. In addition to this, Christopher Alam also speaks in churches and conferences in the United States and all over the world, with God confirming the preaching and teaching of His Word through accompanying signs.

Christopher Alam may be contacted at:

Dynamis World Ministries
2384 New Holland Pike
Lancaster, PA 17601
Telephone: 717-656-0362
E-mail: dynamis-usa@pentecostalfire.com
Web site: www.pentecostalfire.com